POETRY PLEASE!

POETRY PLEASE!

A SELECTION *of* POPULAR POEMS *from the* RADIO 4 SERIES

Edited by SUSAN ROBERTS

BBC BOOKS

I would like to thank my predecessor, Margaret Bradley, who was responsible with the late Brian Patten for the inception of *Poetry Please!*, for her help, encouragement and enthusiasm for poetry. My thanks also go to Linda Sommer, who has worked on the series with me since 1988, and to Hilary Field for her more recent help.

Over 90 of the poems in this book are available on a BBC Radio Collection double cassette, *Poetry Please! Volume II*, ISBN 0 563 40849 9. The readers are Tim Piggott-Smith, Andrew Sachs, Elizabeth Bell, Rosalind Shanks, Denys Hawthorne and Ronald Pickup.

Published by BBC Books,
a division of BBC Enterprises Limited,
Woodlands, 80 Wood Lane, London W12 0TT
First published 1991
Reprinted 1991 and 1992
Compilation ©BBC Books 1991
Introduction © Susan Roberts 1991
Poems © Individual copyright holders

ISBN 0 563 36160 3

Set in 11/13 pt Garamond Roman by
Ace Filmsetting Ltd, Frome, Somerset
Printed and bound in Great Britain by
Clays Ltd, St Ives PLC, England
Jacket printed by Belmont Press Ltd, Northampton

CONTENTS

5

6

INTRODUCTION

Poetry Please! is unique. It is a popular poetry request programme, and represents the most democratic selection of poetry
on the radio. This is the third *Poetry Please!* anthology, and, like
its predecessors, it contains some of the most frequently
requested poems from the past ten years.

Poetry Please! was first broadcast in October 1979. It began as a
ten-minute programme of requests introduced by a different
poet each month. In April 1989 the programme was given an
extra ten minutes and Simon Rae became the regular presenter.
Contemporary poets still take part in the programme, coming
into the studio to read and discuss their own work, and to intro-
duce the Poem of the Week. Some popular poems by previous
studio guests are included in this anthology, for example, 'The
Mountaineers', by Dannie Abse, 'I am the Great Sun', by Charles
Causley, and 'Engineers' Corner', by Wendy Cope.

I have been producing the programme since 1988, and con-
tinue to be impressed by the volume of our correspondence. We
receive over two hundred letters a month. The requests are
entered onto a computer, and at the moment we have over 7000
poems listed. Many of the poems have been asked for more than
once. Every week I try to include one popular classic as the Poem
of the Week, at least one piece of contemporary work, and one
poem that will be unknown to most listeners. This variety is
reflected in the choice of poems for this book. Here, as in the
programme, you will find W. H. Auden rubbing shoulders with
J. W. Riley, Shelley alongside Edith Nesbit, and John Greenleaf
Whittier within hailing distance of W. B. Yeats.

Not all the poems in this book can be described as great
poetry, but each one has communicated something particular
and valuable to those who have taken the trouble to write in.
Poetry Please! appeals to a wide range of people. We have had
requests from seven-year-olds, and from eighty-seven-year-

olds. One eighty-year-old lady sent in a poem she had learnt at school, written on thirteen sides of notebook-sized paper. Other people's memories have not served them so well. We often get letters from people who want to hear a poem from which they can remember only a single tantalising line.

Another feature of the longer programme is an open invitation to listeners to come on *Poetry Please!* to talk about their choices. This has given us the opportunity to meet and talk to the people who write in, and has led to some intriguing stories and some interesting discoveries. Often a poem dug up from obscurity strikes a powerful chord with the audience. When one listener, Colin MacLeod, introduced and read 'Macallister Dances Before the King', by D. M. Mackenzie, the response was so great that I had no hesitation in including the poem here.

No sketch of the programme would be complete without mention of our excellent readers, whose versatile interpretations bring requested poems to life, week after week. Like the radio programme, this anthology is designed to appeal to all lovers of poetry. Whether you are a regular listener or not, I hope you enjoy it.

Susan Roberts
Producer

POETRY PLEASE!

Simon Rae

Requests come in in sackfuls
 Sent in from near and far;
From Aberdeen and Bridlington,
 From Stroud or Potters Bar.

Some are typed with margins
 Luxuriously wide,
And some are scrawled on notepad sheets
 And have a stamp inside.

Some listeners remember
 The lines they learnt at school
And write them out in copperplate
 As straight as any rule.

Others aren't so helpful,
 And scribble on a card
A half-line they can half recall
 – Which makes our job quite hard.

Some enjoy the classics,
 But not the modern stuff,
And when they hear me rabbit on
 They cry, 'That's quite enough!'

Some like Dylan Thomas,
 And some like Dr Donne;
Some idolise Romantic verse,
 And some think nonsense fun.

Each programme is a mixture,
With, let's say, Chesterton
Alongside Greenleaf Whittier,
Shakespeare and Anon.

You can't please all the people,
As has been truly said,
But do, please, keep on writing in.
Your every letter's read.

Dannie Abse 1923–

THE MOUNTAINEERS

Despite the drums we were ready to go.
The natives warned us shaking their spears.
Soon we'd look down on them a mile below
rather as Icarus, so many poets ago,
waved to those shy, forlorn ones, dumb on a thumbnail field.
We started easily but oh the climb was slow.

Above us, the grey perilous rocks like our pride
rose higher and higher – broken teeth of the mountain –
while below the dizzy cliffs, the tipsy angles signified
breathless vertigo and falling possible suicide.
So we climbed on, roped together. At the night camps
our voices babel yet our journey glorified.

The soul too has altitudes and the great birds fly
over. All the summer long we climbed higher,
crag above crag under a copper sulphate sky,
peak above peak singing of the deserted, shy,
inconsolable ones. Still we climb to the chandelier stars
and the more we sing the more we die.

So ascending in that high Sinai of the air,
in space and canyons of the spirit, we lost ourselves
amongst the animals of the mountain – the terrible stare
of self meeting itself – and no one would dare
return, descend to that most flat and average world.
Rather, we made a small faith out of a tall despair.

Shakespeare, Milton, Wordsworth, came this way
near the lonely precipice, their faces gold
in the marigold sunset. But they could never stay
under the hurricane tree so climbed to allay
that voice which cried: 'You many never climb again.'
Our faces too are gold but our feet are clay.

We discovered more than footprints in the snow,
more than mountain ghost, more than desolate glory,
yet now, looking down, we see nothing below
except wind, steaming ice, floating mist – and so
silently, sadly, we follow higher the rare songs of oxygen.
The more we climb the further we have to go.

QUEEN NEFERTITI

Spin a coin, spin a coin,
   All fall down;
Queen Nefertiti
   Stalks through the town.

Over the pavements
   Her feet go clack
Her legs are as tall
   As a chimney stack;

Her fingers flicker
   Like snakes in the air,
The walls split open
   At her green-eyed stare;

Her voice is thin
   As the ghosts of bees;
She will crumble your bones,
   She will make your blood freeze.

Spin a coin, spin a coin,
   All fall down;
Queen Nefertiti
   Stalks through the town.

REMONSTRANCE WITH THE SNAILS

Ye little snails,
With slippery tails,
Who noiselessly travel
Along this gravel,
By a silvery path of slime unsightly,
I learn that you visit my pea-rows nightly.
Felonious your visit, I guess!
And I give you this warning,
That, every morning,
I'll strictly examine the pods;
And if one I hit on,
With slaver or spit on,
Your next meal will be with the gods.

I own you're a very ancient race,
And Greece and Babylon were amid;
You have tenanted many a royal dome,
And dwelt in the oldest pyramid;
The source of the Nile! – O, you have been there!
In the ark was your floodless bed;
On the moonless night of Marathon
You crawled o'er the mighty dead;
But still, though I reverence your ancestries,
I don't see why you should nibble my peas.

The meadows are yours, – the hedgerow and brook,
You may bathe in their dews at morn;
By the aged sea you may sound your *shells*,
On the mountains erect your *horn*;

16

The fruits and the flowers are your rightful dowers,
    Then why – in the name of wonder –
Should my six pea-rows be the only cause
    To excite your midnight plunder!

I have never disturbed your slender shells;
    You have hung round my aged walk;
And each might have sat, till he died in his fat,
    Beneath his own cabbage-stalk:
But now you must fly from the soil of your sires;
    Then put on your liveliest crawl,
And think of your poor little snails at home,
    Now orphans or emigrants all.

    Utensils domestic and civil and social
        I give you an evening to pack up;
But if the moon of this night does not rise
            on your flight,
        Tomorrow I'll hang each man Jack up.
    You'll think of my peas and your thievish tricks,
    With tears of slime, when crossing the *Styx*.

SIR PATRICK SPENS

The king sits in Dumferling toune,
   Drinking the blude-reid wine:
'O whar will I get guid sailor,
   To sail this schip of mine?'

Up and spak an eldern knicht,
   Sat at the kings richt kne:
'Sir Patrick Spence is the best sailor
   That sails upon the se.'

The king has written a braid letter,
   And signed wi' his hand,
And sent it to Sir Patrick Spence,
   Was walking on the sand.

The first line that Sir Patrick red,
   A loud lauch lauched he;
The next line that Sir Patrick red,
   The teir blinded his ee.

'O wha is this has done this deid,
   This ill deid don to me,
To send me out this time o' the yeir,
   To sail upon the se?'

'Mak hast, mak hast, my mirry men all,
   Our guid schip sails the morne:'
'O say na sae, my master deir,
   For I feir a deadlie storme.'

'Late late yestreen I saw the new moone,
  Wi' the auld moone in hir arme,
And I feir, I feir, my deir master,
  That we will cum to harme.'

O our Scots nobles were rich laith
  To weet their cork-heild schoone;
Bot lang owre a' the play wer playd,
  Thair hats they swam aboone.

O lang, lang, may their ladies sit,
  Wi' thair fans into their hand,
Or eir they se Sir Patrick Spence
  Cum sailing to the land.

O lang, lang, may the ladies stand,
  Wi' thair gold kems in their hair,
Waiting for their ain deir lords,
  For they'll se thame na mair.

Have owre, have owre to Aberdour,
  It's fifty fadom deip,
And thair lies guid Sir Patrick Spence,
  Wi' the Scots lords at his feit.

DOVER BEACH

The sea is calm to-night.
The tide is full, the moon lies fair
Upon the straits; – on the French coast the light
Gleams and is gone; the cliffs of England stand,
Glimmering and vast, out in the tranquil bay.
Come to the window, sweet is the night-air!
Only, from the long line of spray
Where the sea meets the moon-blanched land,
Listen! you hear the grating roar
Of pebbles which the waves draw back, and fling,
At their return, up the high strand,
Begin, and cease, and then again begin,
With tremulous cadence slow, and bring
The eternal note of sadness in.

Sophocles long ago
Heard it on the Ægæan, and it brought
Into his mind the turbid ebb and flow
Of human misery; we
Find also in the sound a thought,
Hearing it by this distant northern sea.

The Sea of Faith
Was once, too, at the full, and round earth's shore
Lay like the folds of a bright girdle furled.
But now I only hear
Its melancholy, long, withdrawing roar,
Retreating, to the breath
Of the night-wind, down the vast edges drear
And naked shingles of the world.

Ah, love, let us be true
To one another! for the world, which seems
To lie before us like a land of dreams,
So various, so beautiful, so new,
Hath really neither joy, nor love, nor light,
Nor certitude, nor peace, nor help for pain;
And we are here as on a darkling plain
Swept with confused alarms of struggle and flight,
Where ignorant armies clash by night.

LULLABY

Lay your sleeping head, my love,
Human on my faithless arm;
Time and fevers burn away
Individual beauty from
Thoughtful children, and the grave
Proves the child ephemeral:
But in my arms till break of day
Let the living creature lie,
Mortal, guilty, but to me
The entirely beautiful.

Soul and body have no bounds:
To lovers as they lie upon
Her tolerant enchanted slope
In their ordinary swoon,
Grave the vision Venus sends
Of supernatural sympathy,
Universal love and hope;
While an abstract insight wakes
Among the glaciers and the rocks
The hermit's carnal ecstasy.

Certainty, fidelity
On the stroke of midnight pass
Like vibrations of a bell
And fashionable madmen raise
Their pedantic boring cry:

Every farthing of the cost,
All the dreaded cards foretell,
Shall be paid, but from this night
Not a whisper, not a thought,
Not a kiss nor look be lost.

Beauty, midnight, vision dies:
Let the winds of dawn that blow
Softly round your dreaming head
Such a day of welcome show
Eye and knocking heart may bless,
Find our mortal world enough;
Noons of dryness find you fed
By the involuntary powers,
Nights of insult let you pass
Watched by every human love.

THE WIFE A-LOST

Since I noo mwore do zee your feäce,
    Up steäirs or down below,
I'll zit me in the lwonesome pleäce
    Where flat-bough'd beech do grow:
Below the beeches' bough, my love,
    Where you did never come,
An' I don't look to meet ye now,
    As I do look at hwome.

Since you noo mwore be at my zide,
    In walks in zummer het,
I'll goo alwone where mist do ride,
    Drough trees a drippèn wet:
Below the raïn-wet bough, my love,
    Where you did never come,
An' I don't grieve to miss ye now,
    As I do grieve at hwome.

Since now bezide my dinner-bwoard
    Your vaïce do never sound,
I'll eat the bit I can avword
    A-vield upon the ground;
Below the darksome bough, my love,
    Where you did never dine,
An' I don't grieve to miss ye now,
    As I at hwome do pine.

Since I do miss your vaïce an' feäce
   In praÿer at eventide,
I'll praÿ wi' woone sad vaïce vor greäce
   To goo where you do bide;
Above the tree an' bough, my love,
   Where you be gone avore,
An' be a waïtèn vor me now,
   To come vor evermwore.

CHRISTMAS

The bells of waiting Advent ring,
　The Tortoise stove is lit again
And lamp-oil light across the night
　Has caught the streaks of winter rain
In many a stained-glass window sheen
From Crimson Lake to Hooker's Green.

The holly in the windy hedge
　And round the Manor House the yew
Will soon be stripped to deck the ledge,
　The altar, font and arch and pew,
So that the villagers can say
'The church looks nice' on Christmas Day.

Provincial public houses blaze
　And Corporation tramcars clang,
On lighted tenements I gaze
　Where paper decorations hang,
And bunting in the red Town Hall
Says 'Merry Christmas to you all.'

And London shops on Christmas Eve
　Are strung with silver bells and flowers
As hurrying clerks the City leave
　To pigeon-haunted classic towers,
And marbled clouds go scudding by
The many-steepled London sky.

And girls in slacks remember Dad,
 And oafish louts remember Mum,
And sleepless children's hearts are glad,
 And Christmas-morning bells say 'Come!'
Even to shining ones who dwell
Safe in the Dorchester Hotel.

And is it true? And is it true,
 This most tremendous tale of all,
Seen in a stained-glass window's hue,
 A Baby in an ox's stall?
The Maker of the stars and sea
Become a Child on earth for me?

And is it true? For if it is,
 No loving fingers tying strings
Around those tissued fripperies,
 The sweet and silly Christmas things,
Bath salts and inexpensive scent
And hideous tie so kindly meant,

No love that in a family dwells,
 No carolling in frosty air,
Nor all the steeple-shaking bells
 Can with this single Truth compare –
That God was Man in Palestine
And lives to-day in Bread and Wine.

Laurence Binyon 1869–1943

THE LITTLE DANCERS

Lonely, save for a few faint stars, the sky
Dreams; and lonely, below, the little street
Into its gloom retires, secluded and shy.
Scarcely the dumb roar enters this soft retreat;
And all is dark, save where come flooding rays
From a tavern-window; there, to the brisk measure
Of an organ that down in an alley merrily plays,
Two children, all alone and no one by,
Holding their tattered frocks, thro' an airy maze
Of motion lightly threaded with nimble feet
Dance sedately; face to face they gaze,
Their eyes shining, grave with a perfect pleasure.

Edmund Blunden 1896–1974

FOREFATHERS

Here they went with smock and crook,
    Toiled in the sun, lolled in the shade,
Here they mudded out the brook
    And here their hatchet cleared the glade:
Harvest-supper woke their wit,
Huntsman's moon their wooings lit.

From this church they led their brides,
    From this church themselves were led
Shoulder-high; on these waysides
    Sat to take their beer and bread.
Names are gone – what men they were
    These their cottages declare.

Names are vanished, save the few
    In the old brown Bible scrawled;
These were men of pith and thew,
    Whom the city never called;
Scarce could read or hold a quill,
Built the barn, the forge, the mill.

On the green they watched their sons
    Playing till too dark to see,
As their fathers watched them once,
    As my father once watched me;
While the bat and beetle flew
On the warm air webbed with dew.

Unrecorded, unrenowned,
    Men from whom my ways begin,
Here I know you by your ground
    But I know you not within –
There is silence, there survives
Not a moment of your lives.

Like the bee that now is blown
    Honey-heavy on my hand,
From his toppling tansy-throne
    In the green tempestuous land –
I'm in clover now, nor know
Who made honey long ago.

Robert Bridges 1844–1930

LONDON SNOW

When men were all asleep the snow came flying,
In large white flakes falling on the city brown,
Stealthily and perpetually settling and loosely lying,
  Hushing the latest traffic of the drowsy town;
Deadening, muffling, stifling its murmurs failing;
Lazily and incessantly floating down and down;
  Silently sifting and veiling road, roof and railing;
Hiding difference, making unevenness even,
Into angles and crevices softly drifting and sailing.
  All night it fell, and when full inches seven
It lay in the depth of its uncompacted lightness,
The clouds blew off from a high and frosty heaven;
  And all woke earlier for the unaccustomed brightness
Of the winter dawning, the strange unheavenly glare:
The eye marvelled – marvelled at the dazzling whiteness;
  The ear hearkened to the stillness of the solemn air;
No sound of wheel rumbling nor of foot falling,
And the busy morning cries came thin and spare.
  Then boys I heard, as they went to school, calling,
They gathered up the crystal manna to freeze
Their tongues with tasting, their hands with snowballing;
  Or rioted in a drift, plunging up to the knees;
Or peering up from under the white-mossed wonder,
'O look at the trees!' they cried, 'O look at the trees!'
  With lessened load a few carts creak and blunder,
Following along the white deserted way,
A country company long dispersed asunder:
  When now already the sun, in pale display
Standing by Paul's high dome, spread forth below
His sparkling beams, and awoke the stir of the day.

For now doors open, and war is waged with the snow;
And trains of sombre men, past tale of number,
Tread long brown paths, as toward their toil they go:
But even for them awhile no cares encumber
Their minds diverted; the daily word is unspoken,
The daily thoughts of labour and sorrow slumber
At the sight of the beauty that greets them, for the charm
they have broken.

Anne Brontë 1820–49

―――――――――

LINES COMPOSED IN A WOOD ON A WINDY DAY

My soul is awakened, my spirit is soaring,
And carried aloft on the wings of the breeze;
For, above, and around me, the wild wind is roaring
Arousing to rapture the earth and the seas.

The long withered grass in the sunshine is glancing,
The bare trees are tossing their branches on high;
The dead leaves beneath them are merrily dancing,
The white clouds are scudding across the blue sky.

I wish I could see how the ocean is lashing
The foam of its billows to whirlwinds of spray,
I wish I could see how its proud waves are dashing
And hear the wild roar of their thunder today!

'A LITTLE WHILE'

A little while, a little while
The noisy crowd are barred away;
And I can sing and I can smile –
A little while I've holiday!

Where wilt thou go, my harassed heart?
Full many a land invites thee now;
And places near, and far apart
Have rest for thee, my weary brow.

There is a spot 'mid barren hills
Where winter howls and driving rain,
But if the dreary tempest chills
There is a light that warms again.

The house is old, the trees are bare
And moonless bends the misty dome
But what on earth is half so dear –
So longed for as the hearth of home?

The mute bird sitting on the stone,
The dank moss dripping from the wall,
The garden-walk with weeds o'ergrown,
I love them – how I love them all!

Shall I go there? or shall I seek
Another clime, another sky,
Where tongues familiar music speak
In accents dear to memory?

Yes, as I mused, the naked room,
The flickering firelight died away
And from the midst of cheerless gloom
I passed to bright, unclouded day –

A little and a lone green lane
That opened on a common wide;
A distant, dreamy, dim blue chain
Of mountains circling every side –

A heaven so clear, an earth so calm,
So sweet, so soft, so hushed an air
And, deepening still the dream-like charm,
Wild moor-sheep feeding everywhere –

That was the scene – I knew it well,
I knew the pathways far and near
That winding o'er each billowy swell
Marked out the tracks of wandering deer.

Could I have lingered but an hour
It well had paid a week of toil
But truth has banished fancy's power
I hear my dungeon bars recoil –

Even as I stood with raptured eye
Absorbed in bliss so deep and dear
My hour of rest had fleeted by
And given me back to weary care.

_____

SONNET: 'OH! DEATH WILL FIND ME'

Oh! Death will find me, long before I tire
   Of watching you; and swing me suddenly
Into the shade and loneliness and mire
   Of the last land! There, waiting patiently,

One day, I think, I'll feel a cool wind blowing,
   See a slow light across the Stygian tide,
And hear the Dead about me stir, unknowing,
   And tremble. And *I* shall know that you have died,

And watch you, a broad-browed and smiling dream,
   Pass, light as ever, through the lightless host,
Quietly ponder, start, and sway, and gleam –
   Most individual and bewildering ghost! –

And turn, and toss your brown delightful head
Amusedly, among the ancient Dead.

Elizabeth Barrett Browning 1806–61

SONNET XLIII: 'HOW DO I LOVE THEE?'

How do I love thee? Let me count the ways.
I love thee to the depth and breadth and height
My soul can reach, when feeling out of sight
For the ends of Being and ideal Grace.
I love thee to the level of everyday's
Most quiet need, by sun and candlelight.
I love thee freely, as men strive for Right;
I love thee purely, as they turn from Praise.
I love thee with the passion put to use
In my old griefs, and with my childhood's faith.
I love thee with a love I seemed to lose
With my lost saints, – I love thee with the breath,
Smiles, tears, of all my life! – and, if God choose,
I shall but love thee better after death.

PORPHYRIA'S LOVER

The rain set early in to-night,
    The sullen wind was soon awake,
It tore the elm-tops down for spite,
    And did its worst to vex the lake:
    I listened with heart fit to break.
When glided in Porphyria; straight
    She shut the cold out and the storm,
And kneeled and made the cheerless grate
    Blaze up, and all the cottage warm;
    Which done, she rose, and from her form
Withdrew the dripping cloak and shawl,
    And laid her soiled gloves by, untied
Her hat and let the damp hair fall,
    And, last, she sat down by my side
    And called me. When no voice replied,
She put my arm about her waist,
    And made her smooth white shoulder bare,
And all her yellow hair displaced,
    And stooping, made my cheek lie there,
    And spread, o'er all, her yellow hair,
Murmuring how she loved me – she
    Too weak, for all her heart's endeavour,
To set its struggling passion free
    From pride, and vainer ties dissever,
    And give herself to me for ever.
But passion sometimes would prevail,
    Nor could to-night's gay feast restrain
A sudden thought of one so pale
    For love of her, and all in vain:
    So, she was come through wind and rain.

Be sure I looked up at her eyes
    Happy and proud; at last I knew
Porphyria worshipped me; surprise
    Made my heart swell, and still it grew
    While I debated what to do.
That moment she was mine, mine, fair,
    Perfectly pure and good: I found
A thing to do, and all her hair
    In one long yellow string I wound
    Three times her little throat around,
And strangled her. No pain felt she;
    I am quite sure she felt no pain.
As a shut bud that holds a bee,
    I warily oped her lids: again
    Laughed the blue eyes without a stain.
And I untightened next the tress
    About her neck; her cheek once more
Blushed bright beneath my burning kiss:
    I propped her head up as before,
    Only, this time my shoulder bore
Her head, which droops upon it still:
    The smiling rosy little head,
So glad it has its utmost will,
    That all it scorned at once is fled,
    And I, its love, am gained instead!
Porphyria's love: she guessed not how
    Her darling one wish would be heard.
And thus we sit together now,
    And all night long we have not stirred,
    And yet God has not said a word!

George Gordon, Lord Byron 1788–1824

THE EVE OF WATERLOO
From 'Childe Harold's Pilgrimage'

There was a sound of revelry by night,
   And Belgium's Capital had gathered then
   Her Beauty and her Chivalry, and bright
   The lamps shone o'er fair women and brave men;
   A thousand hearts beat happily; and when
   Music arose with its voluptuous swell,
   Soft eyes looked love to eyes which spake again,
   And all went merry as a marriage bell;
But hush! hark! a deep sound strikes like a rising knell!

Did ye not hear it? – No; 'twas but the wind,
   Or the car rattling o'er the stony street;
   On with the dance! let joy by unconfined;
   No sleep till morn, when Youth and Pleasure meet
   To chase the glowing Hours with flying feet –
   But hark! – that heavy sound breaks in once more,
   As if the clouds its echo would repeat;
   And nearer, clearer, deadlier than before!
Arm! Arm! it is – it is – the cannon's opening roar!

Within a windowed niche of that high hall
   Sate Brunswick's fated chieftain; he did hear
   That sound the first amidst the festival,
   And caught its tone with Death's prophetic ear;
   And when they smiled because he deemed it near,
   His heart more truly knew that peal too well
   Which stretched his father on a bloody bier,
   And roused the vengeance blood alone could quell;
He rushed into the field, and, foremost fighting, fell.

Ah! then and there was hurrying to and fro,
  And gathering tears, and tremblings of distress,
  And cheeks all pale, which but an hour ago
  Blushed at the praise of their own loveliness;
  And there were sudden partings, such as press
  The life from out young hearts, and choking sighs
  Which ne'er might be repeated; who could guess
  If ever more should meet those mutual eyes,
Since upon night so sweet such awful morn could rise!

And there was mounting in hot haste: the steed,
  The mustering squadron, and the clattering car,
  Went pouring forward with impetuous speed,
  And swiftly forming in the ranks of war;
  And the deep thunder peal on peal afar;
  And near, the beat of the alarming drum
  Roused up the soldier ere the morning star;
  While thronged the citizens with terror dumb,
Or whispering, with white lips – 'The foe! They come!
    they come!'

And wild and high the 'Cameron's Gathering' rose!
  The war-note of Lochiel, which Albyn's hills
  Have heard, and heard, too, have her Saxon foes: –
  How in the noon of night that pibroch thrills,
  Savage and shrill! But with the breath which fills
  Their mountain-pipe, so fill the mountaineers
  With the fierce native daring which instils
  The stirring memory of a thousand years,
And Evan's Donald's fame rings in each clansman's ears!

And Ardennes waves above them her green leaves,
  Dewy with nature's tear-drops, as they pass,
  Grieving, if aught inanimate e'er grieves,
  Over the unreturning brave, – alas!

Ere evening to be trodden like the grass
Which now beneath them, but above shall grow
In its next verdure, when this fiery mass
Of living valour, rolling on the foe
And burning with high hope, shall moulder cold and low.

Last noon beheld them full of lusty life,
Last eve in Beauty's circle proudly gay,
The midnight brought the signal-sound of strife,
The morn the marshalling in arms, – the day
Battle's magnificently-stern array!
The thunder-clouds close o'er it, which when rent
The earth is covered thick with other clay
Which her own clay shall cover, heaped and pent,
Rider and horse, – friend, foe, – in one red burial blent!

Ray Campbell 1901–57

HORSES ON THE CAMARGUE

In the grey wastes of dread,
The haunt of shattered gulls where nothing moves
But in a shroud of silence like the dead,
I heard a sudden harmony of hooves,
And, turning, saw afar
A hundred snowy horses unconfined,
The silver runaways of Neptune's car
Racing, spray-curled, like waves before the wind.
Sons of the Mistral, fleet
As him with whose strong gusts they love to flee,
Who shod the flying thunders on their feet
And plunged them with the snortings of the sea;
Theirs is no earthly breed
Who only haunt the verges of the earth
And only on the sea's salt herbage feed –
Surely the great white breakers gave them birth.
For when for years a slave,
A horse of the Camargue, in alien lands,
Should catch some far-off fragrance of the wave
Carried far inland from his native sands,
Many have told the tale
Of how in fury, foaming at the rein,
He hurls his rider; and with lifted tail,
With coal-red eyes and cataracting mane,
Heading his course for home,
Though sixty foreign leagues before him sweep,
Will never rest until he breathes the foam
And hears the native thunder of the deep.
But when the great gusts rise
And lash their anger on these arid coasts,

When the scared gulls career with mournful cries
And whirl across the waste like driven ghosts:
When hail and fire converge,
The only souls to which they strike no pain
Are the white-crested fillies of the surge
And the white horses of the windy plain.
Then in their strength and pride
The stallions of the wilderness rejoice;
They feel their Master's trident in their side,
And high and shrill they answer to his voice.
With white tails smoking free,
Long streaming manes, and arching necks, they show
Their kinship to their sisters of the sea –
And forward hurl their thunderbolts of snow.
Still out of hardship bred,
Spirits of power and beauty and delight
Have ever on such frugal pastures fed
And loved to course with tempests through the night.

Charles Causley 1917–

—————

I AM THE GREAT SUN
From a Normandy crucifix of 1632

I am the great sun, but you do not see me,
   I am your husband, but you turn away.
I am the captive, but you do not free me,
   I am the captain you will not obey.

I am the truth, but you will not believe me,
   I am the city where you will not stay,
I am your wife, your child, but you will leave me,
   I am that God to whom you will not pray.

I am your counsel, but you do not hear me,
   I am the lover whom you will betray,
I am the victor, but you do not cheer me,
   I am the holy dove whom you will slay.

I am your life, but if you will not name me,
Seal up your soul with tears, and never blame me.

C. P. Cavafy 1863–1933

——————————

WAITING FOR THE BARBARIANS

What are we waiting for, assembled in the forum?

    The barbarians are due here today.

Why isn't anything going on in the senate?
Why are the senators sitting there without legislating?

    Because the barbarians are coming today.
    What's the point of senators making laws now?
    Once the barbarians are here, they'll do the legislating.

Why did our emperor get up so early,
and why is he sitting enthroned at the city's main gate,
in state, wearing the crown?

    Because the barbarians are coming today
    and the emperor's waiting to receive their leader.
    He's even got a scroll to give him,
    loaded with titles, with imposing names.

Why have our two consuls and praetors come out today
wearing their embroidered, their scarlet togas?
Why have they put on bracelets with so many amethysts,
rings sparkling with magnificent emeralds?
Why are they carrying elegant canes
beautifully worked in silver and gold?

    Because the barbarians are coming today
    and things like that dazzle the barbarians.

Why don't our distinguished orators turn up as usual
to make their speeches, say what they have to say?

Because the barbarians are coming today
and they're bored by rhetoric and public speaking.

Why this sudden bewilderment, this confusion?
(How serious people's faces have become.)
Why are the streets and squares emptying so rapidly,
everyone going home lost in thought?

Because night has fallen and the barbarians haven't come.
And some of our men just in from the border say
there are no barbarians any longer.

Now what's going to happen to us without barbarians?
Those people were a kind of solution.

THE DONKEY

When fishes flew and forests walked
   And figs grew upon thorn,
Some moment when the moon was blood
   Then surely I was born.

With monstrous head and sickening cry
   And ears like errant wings,
The devil's walking parody
   On all four-footed things.

The tattered outlaw of the earth,
   Of ancient crooked will;
Starve, scourge, deride me: I am dumb,
   I keep my secret still.

Fools! For I also had my hour;
   One far fierce hour and sweet:
There was a shout about my ears,
   And palms before my feet.

John Clare 1793–1864

THE THRUSHES NEST

Within a thick and spreading awthorn bush
That overhung a molehill large and round
I heard from morn to morn a merry thrush
Sing hymns to sunrise while I drank the sound
With joy and often an intruding guest
I watched her secret toils from day to day
How true she warped the moss to form her nest
And modelled it within with wood and clay
And bye and bye like heath bells gilt with dew
There lay her shining eggs as bright as flowers
Ink-spotted over shells of greeny blue
And there I witnessed in the summer hours
A brood of natures minstrels chirp and fly
Glad as the sunshine and the laughing sky

Elizabeth Coatsworth 1893–

ON A NIGHT OF SNOW

Cat, if you go outdoors, you must walk in the snow.
You will come back with little white shoes on your feet,
little white shoes of snow that have heels of sleet.
Stay by the fire, my Cat. Lie still, do not go.
See how the flames are leaping and hissing low,
I will bring you a saucer of milk like a marguerite,
so white and so smooth, so spherical and so sweet –
stay with me, Cat. Outdoors the wild winds blow.

Outdoors the wild winds blow, Mistress, and dark is the
        night,
strange voices cry in the trees, intoning strange lore,
and more than cats move, lit by our eyes' green light,
on silent feet where the meadow grasses hang hoar –
Mistress, there are portents abroad of magic and might,
and things that are yet to be done. Open the door!

Samuel Taylor Coleridge 1772–1834

FROST AT MIDNIGHT

The Frost performs its secret ministry,
Unhelped by any wind. The owlet's cry
Came loud – and hark, again! loud as before.
The inmates of my cottage, all at rest,
Have left me to that solitude, which suits
Abstruser musings: save that at my side
My cradled infant slumbers peacefully.
'Tis calm indeed! so calm, that it disturbs
And vexes meditation with its strange
And extreme silentness. Sea, hill, and wood,
This populous village! Sea, and hill, and wood,
With all the numberless goings-on of life,
Inaudible as dreams! the thin blue flame
Lies on my low-burnt fire, and quivers not;
Only that film, which fluttered on the grate,
Still flutters there, the sole unquiet thing.
Methinks, its motion in this hush of nature
Gives it dim sympathies with me who live,
Making it a companionable form,
Whose puny flaps and freaks the idling Spirit
By its own moods interprets, everywhere
Echo or mirror seeking of itself,
And makes a toy of Thought.

But O! how oft,
How oft, at school, with most believing mind,
Presageful, have I gazed upon the bars,
To watch that fluttering *stranger*! and as oft
With unclosed lids, already had I dreamt
Of my sweet birth-place, and the old church-tower,

Whose bells, the poor man's only music, rang
From morn to evening, all the hot Fair-day,
So sweetly, that they stirred and haunted me
With a wild pleasure, falling on mine ear
Most like articulate sounds of things to come!
So gazed I, till the soothing things I dreamt,
Lulled me to sleep, and sleep prolonged my dreams!
And so I brooded all the following morn,
Awed by the stern preceptor's face, mine eye
Fixed with mock study on my swimming book:
Save if the door half opened, and I snatched
A hasty glance, and still my heart leaped up,
For still I hoped to see the *stranger's* face,
Townsman, or aunt, or sister more beloved,
My play-mate when we both were clothed alike!

Dear Babe, that sleepest cradled by my side,
Whose gentle breathings, heard in this deep calm,
Fill up the interspersèd vacancies
And momentary pauses of the thought!
My babe so beautiful! it thrills my heart
With tender gladness, thus to look at thee,
And think that thou shalt learn far other lore,
And in far other scenes! For I was reared
In the great city, pent 'mid cloisters dim,
And saw nought lovely but the sky and stars.
But *thou*, my babe! shalt wander like a breeze
By lakes and sandy shores, beneath the crags
Of ancient mountain, and beneath the clouds,
Which image in their bulk both lakes and shores
And mountain crags: so shalt thou see and hear
The lovely shapes and sounds intelligible
Of that eternal language, which thy God
Utters, who from eternity doth teach
Himself in all, and all things in himself.

Great universal Teacher! he shall mould
Thy spirit, and by giving make it ask.

Therefore all seasons shall be sweet to thee,
Whether the summer clothe the general earth
With greenness, or the redbreast sit and sing
Betwixt the tufts of snow on the bare branch
Of mossy apple-tree, while the nigh thatch
Smokes in the sun-thaw; whether the eave-drops fall
Heard only in the trances of the blast,
Or if the secret ministry of frost
Shall hang them up in silent icicles,
Quietly shining to the quiet Moon.

Wendy Cope 1945–

ENGINEERS' CORNER

Why isn't there an Engineers' Corner in Westminster Abbey? In Britain
we've always made more fuss of a ballad than a blueprint . . . How many
schoolchildren dream of becoming great engineers?

Advertisement placed in *The Times* by the Engineering Council

We make more fuss of ballads than of blueprints –
That's why so many poets end up rich,
While engineers scrape by in cheerless garrets.
Who needs a bridge or dam? Who needs a ditch?

Whereas the person who can write a sonnet
Has got it made. It's always been the way,
For everybody knows that we need poems
And everybody reads them every day.

Yes, life is hard if you choose engineering –
You're sure to need another job as well;
You'll have to plan your projects in the evenings
Instead of going out. It must be hell.

While well-heeled poets ride around in Daimlers,
You'll burn the midnight oil to earn a crust,
With no hope of a statue in the Abbey,
With no hope, even, of a modest bust.

No wonder small boys dream of writing couplets
And spurn the bike, the lorry and the train.
There's far too much encouragement for poets –
That's why this country's going down the drain.

Frances Cornford 1886–1960

TO A FAT LADY SEEN FROM THE TRAIN

O why do you walk through the fields in gloves,
   Missing so much and so much?
O fat white woman whom nobody loves,
Why do you walk through the fields in gloves,
When the grass is soft as the breast of doves
   And shivering-sweet to the touch?
O why do you walk through the fields in gloves,
   Missing so much and so much?

William Cowper 1731–1800

From 'THE TASK'

Shaggy, and lean, and shrewd, with pointed ears
And tail cropp'd short, half lurcher and half cur –
His dog attends him. Close behind his heel
Now creeps he slow; and now, with many a frisk
Wide-scamp'ring, snatches up the drifted snow
With iv'ry teeth, or ploughs it with his snout;
Then shakes his powder'd coat, and barks for joy.

W. H. Davies 1871–1940

LEISURE

What is this life if, full of care,
We have no time to stand and stare.

No time to stand beneath the boughs
And stare as long as sheep or cows.

No time to see, when woods we pass,
Where squirrels hide their nuts in grass.

No time to see, in broad daylight,
Streams full of stars like skies at night.

No time to turn at Beauty's glance,
And watch her feet, how they can dance.

No time to wait till her mouth can
Enrich that smile her eyes began.

A poor life this if, full of care,
We have no time to stand and stare.

Emily Dickinson 1830–86

'I STARTED EARLY – TOOK MY DOG'

I started Early – Took my Dog –
And visited the Sea –
The Mermaids in the Basement
Came out to look at me –

And Frigates – in the Upper Floor
Extended Hempen Hands –
Presuming Me to be a Mouse –
Aground – upon the Sands –

But no Man moved Me – till the Tide
Went past my simple Shoe –
And past my Apron – and my Belt
And past my Bodice – too –

And made as He would eat me up –
As wholly as a Dew
Upon a Dandelion's Sleeve –
And then – I started – too –

And He – He followed – close behind –
I felt His Silver Heel
Upon my Ankle – Then my Shoes
Would overflow with Pearl –

Until We met the Solid Town –
No One He seemed to know –
And bowing – with a Mighty look –
At me – The Sea withdrew –

———

A HYMN TO GOD THE FATHER

I

Wilt Thou forgive that sin where I begun,
  Which is my sin, though it were done before?
Wilt Thou forgive that sin, through which I run,
  And do run still: though still I do deplore?
    When Thou hast done, Thou hast not done,
      For, I have more.

II

Wilt Thou forgive that sin by which I have won
  Others to sin? and, made my sin their door?
Wilt Thou forgive that sin which I did shun
  A year, or two: but wallowed in, a score?
    When Thou hast done, Thou hast not done,
      For I have more.

III

I have a sin of fear, that when I have spun
  My last thread, I shall perish on the shore;
Swear by Thyself, that at my death Thy son
  Shall shine as He shines now, and heretofore;
    And, having done that, Thou hast done,
      I fear no more.

Ernest Dowson 1867–1900

NON SUM QUALIS ERAM BONAE
SUB REGNO CYNARAE

Last night, ah, yesternight, betwixt her lips and mine
There fell thy shadow, Cynara! thy breath was shed
Upon my soul between the kisses and the wine;
And I was desolate and sick of an old passion,
    Yea, I was desolate and bowed my head:
I have been faithful to thee, Cynara! in my fashion.

All night upon mine heart I felt her warm heart beat,
Night-long within mine arms in love and sleep she lay;
Surely the kisses of her bought red mouth were sweet;
But I was desolate and sick of an old passion,
    When I awoke and found the dawn was gray:
I have been faithful to thee, Cynara! in my fashion.

I have forgot much, Cynara! gone with the wind,
Flung roses, roses riotously with the throng,
Dancing, to put thy pale, lost lilies out of mind;
But I was desolate and sick of an old passion,
    Yea, all the time, because the dance was long:
I have been faithful to thee, Cynara! in my fashion.

I cried for madder music and for stronger wine,
But when the feast is finished and the lamps expire,
Then falls thy shadow, Cynara! the night is thine;
And I am desolate and sick of an old passion,
    Yea, hungry for the lips of my desire:
I have been faithful to thee, Cynara! in my fashion.

BLACKBIRD

He comes on chosen evenings,
My blackbird bountiful, and sings
Over the gardens of the town
Just at the hour the sun goes down.
His flight across the chimneys thick,
By some divine arithmetic,
Comes to his customary stack,
And couches there his plumage black,
And there he lifts his yellow bill,
Kindled against the sunset, till
These suburbs are like Dymock woods
Where music has her solitudes,
And while he mocks the winter's wrong
Rapt on his pinnacle of song,
Figured above our garden plots,
Those are celestial chimney-pots.

T. S. Eliot 1888–1965

SKIMBLESHANKS: THE RAILWAY CAT

There's a whisper down the line at 11.39
When the Night Mail's ready to depart,
Saying 'Skimble where is Skimble has he gone to hunt
     the thimble?
We must find him or the train can't start.'
All the guards and all the porters and the stationmaster's
     daughters
They are searching high and low,
Saying 'Skimble where is Skimble for unless he's very
     nimble
Then the Night Mail just can't go.'
At 11.42 then the signal's nearly due
And the passengers are frantic to a man –
Then Skimble will appear and he'll saunter to the rear:
He's been busy in the luggage van!
    He gives one flash of his glass-green eyes
      And the signal goes 'All Clear!'
    And we're off at last for the northern part
      Of the Northern Hemisphere!

You may say that by and large it is Skimble who's in charge
Of the Sleeping Car Express.
From the driver and the guards to the bagmen playing cards
He will supervise them all, more or less.
Down the corridor he paces and examines all the faces
Of the travellers in the First and in the Third;
He establishes control by a regular patrol
And he'd know at once if anything occurred.
He will watch you without winking and he sees what you
     are thinking

And it's certain that he doesn't approve
Of hilarity and riot, so the folk are very quiet
When Skimble is about and on the move.
    You can play no pranks with Skimbleshanks!
        He's a Cat that cannot be ignored;
    So nothing goes wrong on the Northern Mail
        When Skimbleshanks is aboard.

Oh it's very pleasant when you have found your little den
With your name written up on the door.
And the berth is very neat with a newly folded sheet
And there's not a speck of dust on the floor.
There is every sort of light – you can make it dark or bright;
There's a button that you turn to make a breeze.
There's a funny little basin you're supposed to wash your
            face in
And a crank to shut the window if you sneeze.
Then the guard looks in politely and will ask you very
            brightly
'Do you like your morning tea weak or strong?'
But Skimble's just behind him and was ready to remind
            him,
For Skimble won't let anything go wrong.
    And when you creep into your cosy berth
        And pull up the counterpane,
You are bound to admit that it's very nice
To know that you won't be bothered by mice –
You can leave all that to the Railway Cat,
    The Cat of the Railway Train!

In the middle of the night he is always fresh and bright;
Every now and then he has a cup of tea
With perhaps a drop of Scotch while he's keeping on the
            watch,
Only stopping here and there to catch a flea.

You were fast asleep at Crewe and so you never knew
That he was walking up and down the station;
You were sleeping all the while he was busy at Carlisle,
Where he greets the stationmaster with elation.
But you saw him at Dumfries, where he summons the
      police
If there's anything they ought to know about:
When you get to Gallowgate there you do not have to
      wait –
For Skimbleshanks will help you to get out!
    He gives you a wave of his long brown tail
      Which says: 'I'll see you again!
      You'll meet without fail on the Midnight Mail
      The Cat of the Railway Train.'

THE OLD SHIPS

I have seen old ships sail like swans asleep
Beyond the village which men still call Tyre,
With leaden age o'ercargoed, dipping deep
For Famagusta and the hidden sun
That rings black Cyprus with a lake of fire;
And all those ships were certainly so old
Who knows how oft with squat and noisy gun,
Questing brown slaves or Syrian oranges,
The pirates Genoese
Hell-raked them till they rolled
Blood, water, fruit and corpses up the hold.
But now through friendly seas they softly run,
Painted the mid-sea blue or shore-sea green,
Still patterned with the vine and grapes in gold.

But I have seen,
Pointing her shapely shadows from the dawn
And image tumbled on a rose-swept bay,
A drowsy ship of some yet older day;
And, wonder's breath indrawn,
Thought I – who knows – who knows – but in that same
(Fished up beyond Ææa, patched up new
– Stern painted brighter blue –)
That talkative, bald-headed seaman came
(Twelve patient comrades sweating at the oar)
From Troy's doom-crimson shore,
And with great lies about his wooden horse
Set the crew laughing, and forget his course.

It was so old a ship – who knows, who knows?
– And yet so beautiful, I watched in vain
To see the mast burst open with a rose,
And the whole deck put on its leaves again.

Robert Frost 1874–1963

AFTER APPLE-PICKING

My long two-pointed ladder's sticking through a tree
Toward heaven still,
And there's a barrel that I didn't fill
Beside it, and there may be two or three
Apples I didn't pick upon some bough.
But I am done with apple-picking now.
Essence of winter sleep is on the night,
The scent of apples: I am drowsing off.
I cannot rub the strangeness from my sight
I got from looking through a pane of glass.
I skimmed this morning from the drinking trough
And held against the world of hoary grass.
It melted, and I let it fall and break.
But I was well
Upon my way to sleep before it fell,
And I could tell
What form my dreaming was about to take.
Magnified apples appear and disappear,
Stem end and blossom end,
And every fleck of russet showing clear.
My instep arch not only keeps the ache,
It keeps the pressure of a ladder-round.
I feel the ladder sway as the boughs bend.
And I keep hearing from the cellar bin
The rumbling sound
Of load on load of apples coming in.
For I have had too much
Of apple-picking: I am overtired
Of the great harvest I myself desired
There were ten thousand thousand fruit to touch,

Cherish in hand, lift down, and not let fall.
For all
That struck the earth,
No matter if not bruised or spiked with stubble,
Went surely to the cider-apple heap
As of no worth.
One can see what will trouble
This sleep of mine, whatever sleep it is.
Were he not gone,
The woodchuck could say whether it's like his
Long sleep, as I describe its coming on,
Or just some human sleep.

From 'THE PROPHET'

Then Almitra spoke again and said, And what of
    Marriage, master?
And he answered saying:
You were born together, and together you shall be for
    evermore.
You shall be together when the white wings of death
    scatter your days.
Aye, you shall be together even in the silent memory
    of God.
But let there be spaces in your togetherness.
And let the winds of the heavens dance between you.

Love one another, but make not a bond of love:
Let it rather be a moving sea between the shores of
    your souls.
Fill each other's cup but drink not from one cup.
Give one another of your bread but eat not from the
    same loaf.
Sing and dance together and be joyous, but let each one
    of you be alone,
Even as the strings of a lute are alone though they
    quiver with the same music.

Give your hearts, but not into each other's keeping.
For only the hand of Life can contain your hearts.
And stand together yet not too near together:
For the pillars of the temple stand apart,
And the oak tree and the cypress grow not in each
    other's shadow.

THE VILLAGE PREACHER
From 'The Deserted Village'

Near yonder copse, where once the garden smiled,
And still where many a garden flower grows wild:
There, where a few torn shrubs the place disclose,
The village preacher's modest mansion rose.
A man he was to all the country dear,
And passing rich with forty pounds a year;
Remote from towns he ran his godly race,
Nor e'er had changed, nor wished to change his place;
Unpractised he to fawn, or seek for power,
By doctrines fashioned to the varying hour;
For other aims his heart had learned to prize,
More skilled to raise the wretched than to rise.
His house was known to all the vagrant train,
He chid their wand'rings, but relieved their pain;
The long-remembered beggar was his guest,
Whose beard descending swept his aged breast;
The ruined spendthrift, now no longer proud,
Claimed kindred there, and had his claims allowed;
The broken soldier, kindly bade to stay,
Sat by his fire, and talked the night away;
Wept o'er his wounds, or tales of sorrow done,
Shouldered his crutch, and showed how fields were won.
Pleased with his guests, the good man learned to glow,
And quite forgot their vices in their woe;
Careless their merits, or their faults to scan,
His pity gave ere charity began.

Thus to relieve the wretched was his pride,
And e'en his failings leaned to virtue's side;
But in his duty prompt at every call,
He watched and wept, he prayed and felt, for all.
And, as a bird each fond endearment tries
To tempt its new-fledged offspring to the skies,
He tried each art, reproved each dull delay,
Allured to brighter worlds, and led the way.

Beside the bed where parting life was laid,
And sorrow, guilt, and pain, by turns dismayed,
The revered champion stood. At his control,
Despair and anguish fled the struggling soul;
Comfort came down the trembling wretch to raise,
And his last falt'ring accents whispered praise.

At church, with meek and unaffected grace,
His looks adorned the venerable place;
Truth from his lips prevailed with double sway,
And fools, who came to scoff, remained to pray.
The service passed, around the pious man,
With steady zeal, each honest rustic ran;
E'en children followed with endearing wile,
And plucked his gown, to share the good man's smile.
His ready smile a parent's warmth expressed,
Their welfare pleased him, and their cares distressed;
To them his heart, his love, his griefs were given,
But all his serious thoughts had rest in Heaven.
As some tall cliff, that lifts its awful form,
Swells from the vale, and midway leaves the storm,
Though round its breast the rolling clouds are spread,
Eternal sunshine settles on its head.

Thomas Gray 1716–71

ON A FAVOURITE CAT,
DROWNED IN A TUB OF GOLDFISHES

'Twas on a lofty vase's side,
Where China's gayest art had dyed
   The azure flowers that blow;
Demurest of the tabby kind,
The pensive Selima reclined,
   Gazed on the lake below.

Her conscious tail her joy declared;
The fair round face, the snowy beard,
   The velvet of her paws,
Her coat, that with the tortoise vies,
Her ears of jet, and emerald eyes.
   She saw; and purred applause.

Still had she gazed; but 'midst the tide
Two angel forms were seen to glide,
   The Genii of the stream:
Their scaly armour's Tyrian hue
Through richest purple to the view
   Betrayed a golden gleam.

The hapless Nymph with wonder saw:
A whisker first and then a claw,
   With many an ardent wish,
She stretched in vain to reach the prize.
What female heart can gold despise?
   What Cat's adverse to fish?

Presumptuous Maid! with looks intent
Again she stretched, again she bent,
   Nor knew the gulf between.
(Malignant Fate sat by, and smiled.)
The slipp'ry verge her feet beguiled,
   She tumbled headlong in.

Eight times emerging from the flood
She mewed to every watery god,
   Some speedy aid to send.
No Dolphin came, no Nereid stirred:
Nor cruel *Tom*, nor *Susan* heard.
   A Fav'rite has no friend!

From hence, ye Beauties, undeceived,
Know, one false step is ne'er retrieved,
   And be with caution bold.
Not all that tempts your wand'ring eyes
And heedless hearts, is lawful prize;
   Nor all that glisters, gold.

Thomas Hardy 1840–1928

―――――――

AFTERWARDS

When the Present has latched its postern behind my
    tremulous stay,
  And the May month flaps its glad green leaves like wings,
Delicate-filmed as new-spun silk, will the neighbours say,
  'He was a man who used to notice such things'?

If it be in the dusk when, like an eyelid's soundless blink,
  The dewfall-hawk comes crossing the shades to alight
Upon the wind-warped upland thorn, a gazer may think,
  'To him this must have been a familiar sight.'

If I pass during some nocturnal blackness, mothy and warm,
  When the hedgehog travels furtively over the lawn,
One may say, 'He strove that such innocent creatures should
    come to no harm,
    But he could do little for them; and now he is gone.'

If, when hearing that I have been stilled at last, they stand at
    the door,
  Watching the full-starred heavens that winter sees,
Will this thought rise on those who will meet my face no
    more,
    'He was one who had an eye for such mysteries'?

And will any say when my bell of quittance is heard in the
    gloom,
  And a crossing breeze cuts a pause in its outrollings,
Till they rise again, as they were a new bell's boom,
  'He hears it not now, but used to notice such things'?

74

Seamus Heaney 1939–

―――――――――

DIGGING

Between my finger and my thumb
The squat pen rests; snug as a gun.

Under my window, a clean rasping sound
When the spade sinks into gravelly ground:
My father, digging. I look down

Till his straining rump among the flowerbeds
Bends low, comes up twenty years away
Stooping in rhythm through potato drills
Where he was digging.

The coarse boot nestled on the lug, the shaft
Against the inside knee was levered firmly.
He rooted out tall tops, buried the bright edge deep
To scatter new potatoes that we picked
Loving their cool hardness in our hands.

By God, the old man could handle a spade.
Just like his old man.

My grandfather cut more turf in a day
Than any other man on Toner's bog.
Once I carried him milk in a bottle
Corked sloppily with paper. He straightened up
To drink it, then fell to right away

Nicking and slicing neatly, heaving sods
Over his shoulder, going down and down
For the good turf. Digging.

The cold smell of potato mould, the squelch and slap
Of soggy peat, the curt cuts of an edge
Through living roots awaken in my head.
But I've no spade to follow men like them.

Between my finger and my thumb
The squat pen rests.
I'll dig with it.

Felicia Hemans 1793–1835

CASABIANCA

The boy stood on the burning deck
    Whence all but he had fled;
The flame that lit the battle's wreck
    Shone round him o'er the dead.

Yet beautiful and bright he stood,
    As born to rule the storm –
A creature of heroic blood,
    A proud, though childlike form.

The flames rolled on – he would not go
    Without his father's word;
That father, faint in death below,
    His voice no longer heard.

He called aloud: 'Say, father, say
    If yet my task is done!'
He knew not that the chieftain lay
    Unconscious of his son.

'Speak, father!' once again he cried,
    'If I may yet be gone!'
And but the booming shots replied,
    And fast the flames rolled on.

Upon his brow he felt their breath,
    And in his waving hair,
And looked from that lone post of death
    In still yet brave despair;

And shouted but once more aloud,
    'My father! must I stay?'
While o'er him fast, through sail and shroud,
    The wreathing fires made way.

They wrapt the ship in splendour wild,
    They caught the flag on high,
And streamed above the gallant child
    Like banners in the sky.

There came a burst of thunder-sound –
    The boy – oh! where was he?
Ask of the winds that far around
    With fragments strewed the sea! –

With mast, and helm, and pennon fair,
    That well had borne their part;
But the noblest thing which perished there
    Was that young faithful heart!

VERTUE

Sweet day, so cool, so calm, so bright,
The bridall of the earth and skie:
The dew shall weep thy fall to night;
           For thou must die.

Sweet rose, whose hue angrie and brave
Bids the rash gazer wipe his eye:
Thy root is ever in its grave,
           And thou must die.

Sweet spring, full of sweet dayes and roses,
A box where sweets compacted lie;
My musick shows ye have your closes,
           And all must die.

Onely a sweet and vertuous soul,
Like season'd timber, never gives;
But though the whole world turn to coal,
           Then chiefly lives.

TO DAFFODILS

Fair daffodils, we weep to see
  You haste away so soon;
As yet the early-rising sun
  Has not attained his noon.
    Stay, stay,
    Until the hasting day
      Has run
    But to the evensong;
And, having prayed together, we
  Will go with you along.

We have short time to stay, as you,
  We have as short a spring;
As quick a growth to meet decay,
  As you, or anything.
    We die,
    As your hours do, and dry
      Away,
    Like to the summer's rain;
Or as the pearls of morning's dew
  Ne'er to be found again.

Ralph Hodgson 1871–1962

THE BELLS OF HEAVEN

'Twould ring the bells of Heaven
The wildest peal for years,
If Parson lost his senses
And people came to theirs,
And he and they together
Knelt down with angry prayers
For tamed and shabby tigers
And dancing dogs and bears,
And wretched, blind pit ponies,
And little hunted hares.

Thomas Hood 1799–1845

NO!

No sun – no moon!
No morn – no noon –
No dawn – no dusk – no proper time of day –
No sky – no earthly view –
No distance looking blue –
No road – no street – no 't'other side the way' –
No end to any Row –
No indications where the Crescents go –
No top to any steeple –
No recognitions of familiar people –
No courtesies for showing 'em –
No knowing 'em! –
No travelling at all – no locomotion,
No inkling of the way – no notion –
'No go' – by land or ocean –
No mail – no post –
No news from any foreign coast –
No Park – no Ring – no afternoon gentility –
No company – no nobility –
No warmth, no cheerfulness, no healthful ease,
No comfortable feel in any member –
No shade, no shine, no butterflies, no bees,
No fruits, no flowers, no leaves, no birds –
November!

Gerard Manley Hopkins 1844–89

AS KINGFISHERS CATCH FIRE

As kingfishers catch fire, dragonflies draw flame;
   As tumbled over rim in roundy wells
   Stones ring; like each tucked string tells, each hung bell's
Bow swung finds tongue to fling out broad its name;
Each mortal thing does one thing and the same:
   Deals out that being indoors each one dwells;
   Selves – goes itself; *myself* it speaks and spells,
Crying *What I do is me: for that I came.*

Í say more: the just man justices;
   Keeps gráce: thát keeps all his goings graces;
Acts in God's eye what in God's eye he is –
   Chríst. For Christ plays in ten thousand places,
Lovely in limbs, and lovely in eyes not his
   To the Father through the features of men's faces.

'TELL ME NOT HERE, IT NEEDS NOT SAYING'

Tell me not here, it needs not saying,
   What tune the enchantress plays
In aftermaths of soft September
   Or under blanching mays,
For she and I were long acquainted
   And I knew all her ways.

On russet floors, by waters idle,
   The pine lets fall its cone;
The cuckoo shouts all day at nothing
   In leafy dells alone;
And traveller's joy beguiles in autumn
   Hearts that have lost their own.

On acres of the seeded grasses
   The changing burnish heaves;
Or marshalled under moons of harvest
   Stand still all night the sheaves;
Or beeches strip in storms for winter
   And stain the wind with leaves.

Possess, as I possessed a season,
   The countries I resign,
Where over elmy plains the highway
   Would mount the hills and shine,
And full of shade the pillared forest
   Would murmur and be mine.

For nature, heartless, witless nature,
    Will neither care nor know
What stranger's feet may find the meadow
    And trespass there and go,
Nor ask amid the dews of morning
    If they are mine or no.

Ted Hughes 1930–

HAWK ROOSTING

I sit in the top of the wood, my eyes closed.
Inaction, no falsifying dream
Between my hooked head and hooked feet:
Or in sleep rehearse perfect kills and eat.

The convenience of the high trees!
The air's buoyancy and the sun's ray
Are of advantage to me;
And the earth's face upward for my inspection.

My feet are locked upon the rough bark.
It took the whole of Creation
To produce my foot, my each feather:
Now I hold Creation in my foot

Or fly up, and revolve it all slowly –
I kill where I please because it is all mine.
There is no sophistry in my body:
My manners are tearing off heads –

The allotment of death.
For the one path of my flight is direct
Through the bones of the living.
No arguments assert my right:

The sun is behind me.
Nothing has changed since I began.
My eye has permitted no change.
I am going to keep things like this.

Emyr Humphreys 1919–

FROM FATHER TO SON

There is no limit to the number of times
Your father can come to life, and he is as tender as ever
    he was
And as poor, his overcoat buttoned to the throat,
His face blue from the wind that always blows in the outer
    darkness
He comes toward you, hesitant,
Unwilling to intrude and yet driven at the point of love
To this encounter.

You may think
That love is all that is left of him, but when he comes
He comes with all his winters and all his wounds.
He stands shivering in the empty street,
Cold and worn like a tramp at the end of a journey
And yet a shape of unquestioning love that you
Uneasy and hesitant of the cold touch of death
Must embrace.

Then, before you can touch him
He is gone, leaving on your fingers
A little more of his weariness
A little more of his love.

SONG AT THE BEGINNING OF AUTUMN

Now watch this autumn that arrives
In smells. All looks like summer still;
Colours are quite unchanged, the air
On green and white serenely thrives.
Heavy the trees with growth and full
The fields. Flowers flourish everywhere.

Proust who collected time within
A child's cake would understand
The ambiguity of this –
Summer still raging while a thin
Column of smoke stirs from the land
Proving that autumn gropes for us.

But every season is a kind
Of rich nostalgia. We give names –
Autumn and summer, winter, spring –
As though to unfasten from the mind
Our moods and give them outward forms.
We want the certain, solid thing.

But I am carried back against
My will into a childhood where
Autumn is bonfires, marbles, smoke;
I lean against my window fenced
From evocations in the air.
When I said autumn, autumn broke.

P. J. Kavanagh 1931–

NEWS FROM GLOUCESTERSHIRE

This snow, thaw, frost, thaw and rain
Has bitten great gaps in the old limestone
Walls that summer visitors delighted in:
Dark grey, with rusty orange and sky-grey lichen
And mosses green as cress; they caught the sun
Pink in the morning and, white under the moon,
Shadowed the fox. They have fallen down,

Nor will be, nor should be, built again,
Fences being cheaper; they are done
That were my passion. Foxes' navigation, weasels' run,
Skilful catchers of every light, they open
Like graves, a jumble of yellow bone
That tractors tidy away. Visitors from the town
May vaguely remark an absence, travel on.

The thud, thud, is fence-posts going in.

John Keats 1795–1821

ODE TO A NIGHTINGALE

I

My heart aches, and a drowsy numbness pains
    My sense, as though of hemlock I had drunk,
Or emptied some dull opiate to the drains
    One minute past, and Lethe-wards had sunk:
'Tis not through envy of thy happy lot,
    But being too happy in thine happiness, –
        That thou, light-winged Dryad of the trees,
            In some melodious plot
    Of beechen green, and shadows numberless,
        Singest of summer in full-throated ease.

II

O, for a draught of vintage! that hath been
    Cool'd a long age in the deep-delved earth,
Tasting of Flora and the country green,
    Dance, and Provençal song, and sunburnt mirth!
O for a beaker full of the warm South,
    Full of the true, the blushful Hippocrene,
        With beaded bubbles winking at the brim,
            And purple-stained mouth;
    That I might drink, and leave the world unseen,
        And with thee fade away into the forest dim:

III

Fade far away, dissolve, and quite forget
    What thou among the leaves hast never known,
The weariness, the fever, and the fret
    Here, where men sit and hear each other groan;
Where palsy shakes a few, sad, last gray hairs,

Where youth grows pale, and spectre-thin, and dies;
    Where but to think is to be full of sorrow
        And leaden-eyed despairs,
    Where Beauty cannot keep her lustrous eyes,
        Or new Love pine at them beyond to-morrow.

IV

Away! Away! for I will fly to thee,
    Not charioted by Bacchus and his pards,
But on the viewless wings of Poesy,
    Though the dull brain perplexes and retards:
Already with thee! tender is the night,
    And haply the Queen-Moon is on her throne,
        Cluster'd around by all her starry Fays;
            But here there is no light,
    Save what from heaven is with the breezes blown
        Through verdurous glooms and winding mossy ways.

V

I cannot see what flowers are at my feet,
    Nor what soft incense hangs upon the boughs,
But, in embalmed darkness, guess each sweet
    Wherewith the seasonable month endows
The grass, the thicket, and the fruit-tree wild;
    White hawthorn, and the pastoral eglantine;
        Fast fading violets cover'd up in leaves;
            And mid-May's eldest child,
    The coming musk-rose, full of dewy wine,
        The murmurous haunt of flies on summer eves.

VI

Darkling I listen; and, for many a time
    I have been half in love with easeful Death,
Call'd him soft names in many a mused rhyme,
    To take into the air my quiet breath;

Now more than ever seems it rich to die,
    To cease upon the midnight with no pain,
        While thou art pouring forth thy soul abroad
            In such an ecstasy!
    Still wouldst thou sing, and I have ears in vain –
        To thy high requiem become a sod.

VII

Thou wast not born for death, immortal Bird!
    No hungry generations tread thee down;
The voice I hear this passing night was heard
    In ancient days by emperor and clown:
Perhaps the self-same song that found a path
    Through the sad heart of Ruth, when, sick for home,
        She stood in tears amid the alien corn;
            The same that oft-times hath
    Charm'd magic casements, opening on the foam
        Of perilous seas, in faery lands forlorn.

VIII

Forlorn! the very word is like a bell
    To toll me back from thee to my sole self!
Adieu! the fancy cannot cheat so well
    As she is fam'd to do, deceiving elf.
Adieu! adieu! thy plaintive anthem fades
    Past the near meadows, over the still stream,
        Up the hill-side; and now 'tis buried deep
            In the next valley-glades:
    Was it a vision, or a waking dream?
        Fled is that music: – Do I wake or sleep?

THE SANDS OF DEE

'O Mary, go and call the cattle home,
    And call the cattle home,
    And call the cattle home
  Across the sands of Dee;'
The western wind was wild and dank with foam,
  And all alone went she.

The western tide crept up along the sand,
    And o'er and o'er the sand,
    And round and round the sand,
  As far as eye could see.
The rolling mist came down and hid the land:
  And never home came she.

'Oh! is it weed, or fish, or floating hair –
    A tress of golden hair,
    A drownèd maiden's hair
  Above the nets at sea?
Was never salmon yet that shone so fair
  Among the stakes on Dee.'

They rowed her in across the rolling foam,
    The cruel crawling foam,
    The cruel hungry foam,
  To her grave beside the sea:
But still the boatmen hear her call the cattle home
  Across the sands of Dee.

Rudyard Kipling 1865–1936

EDDI'S SERVICE
(AD 687)
('The Conversion of St. Wilfrid' – *Rewards and Fairies*)

Eddi, priest of St Wilfrid
    In his chapel at Manhood End,
Ordered a midnight service
    For such as cared to attend.

But the Saxons were keeping Christmas,
    And the night was stormy as well.
Nobody came to service,
    Though Eddi rang the bell.

"Wicked weather for walking,'
    Said Eddi of Manhood End.
'But I must go on with the service
    For such as care to attend.'

The altar-lamps were lighted, –
    An old marsh-donkey came,
Bold as a guest invited,
    And stared at the guttering flame.

The storm beat on at the windows,
    The water splashed on the floor,
And a wet, yoke-weary bullock
    Pushed in through the open door.

'How do I know what is greatest,
    How do I know what is least?
That is My Father's business,'
    Said Eddi, Wilfrid's priest.

'But – three are gathered together –
　　Listen to me and attend.
I bring good news, my brethren!'
　　Said Eddi of Manhood End.

And he told the Ox of a Manger
　　And a Stall in Bethlehem,
And he spoke to the Ass of a Rider
　　That rode to Jerusalem.

They steamed and dripped in the chancel,
　　They listened and never stirred,
While, just as though they were Bishops,
　　Eddi preached them The Word,

Till the gale blew off on the marshes
　　And the windows showed the day,
And the Ox and the Ass together
　　Wheeled and clattered away.

And when the Saxons mocked him,
　　Said Eddi of Manhood End,
'I dare not shut His chapel
　　On such as care to attend.'

Philip Larkin 1922–85

_____

CHURCH GOING

Once I am sure there's nothing going on
I step inside, letting the door thud shut.
Another church: matting, seats, and stone,
And little books; sprawlings of flowers, cut
For Sunday, brownish now; some brass and stuff
Up at the holy end; the small neat organ;
And a tense, musty, unignorable silence,
Brewed God knows how long. Hatless, I take off
My cycle-clips in awkward reverence,

Move forward, run my hand around the font.
From where I stand, the roof looks almost new –
Cleaned, or restored? Someone would know: I don't.
Mounting the lectern, I peruse a few
Hectoring large-scale verses, and pronounce
'Here endeth' much more loudly than I'd meant.
The echoes snigger briefly. Back at the door
I sign the book, donate an Irish sixpence,
Reflect the place was not worth stopping for.

Yet stop I did: in fact I often do,
And always end much at a loss like this,
Wondering what to look for; wondering, too,
When churches fall completely out of use
What we shall turn them into, if we shall keep
A few cathedrals chronically on show,
Their parchment, plate and pyx in locked cases,
And let the rest rent-free to rain and sheep.
Shall we avoid them as unlucky places?

Or, after dark, will dubious women come
To make their children touch a particular stone;
Pick simples for a cancer; or on some
Advised night see walking a dead one?
Power of some sort or other will go on
In games, in riddles, seemingly at random;
But superstition, like belief, must die,
And what remains when disbelief has gone?
Grass, weedy pavement, brambles, buttress, sky,

A shape less recognisable each week,
A purpose more obscure. I wonder who
Will be the last, the very last, to seek
This place for what it was; one of the crew
That tap and jot and know what rood-lofts were?
Some ruin-bibber, randy for antique,
Or Christmas-addict, counting on a whiff
Of gown-and-bands and organ-pipes and myrrh?
Or will he be my representative,

Bored, uninformed, knowing the ghostly silt
Dispersed, yet tending to this cross of ground
Through suburb scrub because it held unsplit
So long and equably what since is found
Only in separation – marriage, and birth,
And death, and thoughts of these – for which was built
This special shell? For, though I've no idea
What this accoutred frowsty barn is worth,
It pleases me to stand in silence here;

A serious house on serious earth it is,
In whose blent air all our compulsions meet,
Are recognised, and robed as destinies.
And that much never can be obsolete,

Since someone will forever be surprising
A hunger in himself to be more serious,
And gravitating with it to this ground,
Which, he once heard, was proper to grow wise in,
If only that so many dead lie round.

D. H. Lawrence 1885–1930

―――――――――

BAVARIAN GENTIANS

Not every man has gentians in his house
In soft September, at slow, sad Michaelmas.
Bavarian gentians, tall and dark, but dark
darkening the daytime torch-like with the smoking
    blueness of Pluto's gloom,
ribbed hellish flowers erect, with their blaze of darkness
    spread blue,
blown flat into points, by the heavy white draught of the day.

Torch-flowers of the blue-smoking darkness, Pluto's dark-
    blue blaze
black lamps from the halls of Dis, smoking dark blue
giving off darkness, blue darkness, upon Demeter's yellow-
    pale day
whom have you come for, here in the white-cast day?

Reach me a gentian, give me a torch!
let me guide myself with the blue, forked torch of a flower
down the darker and darker stairs, where blue is darkened
    on blueness
down the way Persephone goes, just now, in first-frosted
    September,
to the sightless realm where darkness is married to dark
and Persephone herself is but a voice, as a bride,
a gloom invisible enfolded in the deeper dark
of the arms of Pluto as he ravishes her once again
and pierces her once more with his passion of the utter dark
among the splendour of black-blue torches, shedding
    fathomless darkness on the nuptials.

Give me a flower on a tall stem, and three dark flames,
for I will go to the wedding, and be wedding-guest
at the marriage of the living dark.

Edward Lear 1812–88

THE OWL AND THE PUSSY-CAT

The Owl and the Pussy-Cat went to sea
   In a beautiful pea-green boat:
They took some honey, and plenty of money
   Wrapped up in a five-pound note.
The Owl looked up to the stars above,
   And sang to a small guitar,
'O lovely Pussy, O Pussy, my love,
   What a beautiful Pussy you are,
         You are,
         You are!
   What a beautiful Pussy you are!'

Pussy said to the Owl, 'You elegant fowl,
   How charmingly sweet you sing!
Oh! let us be married; too long we have tarried:
   But what shall we do for a ring?'
They sailed away, for a year and a day,
   To the land where the bong-tree grows;
And there in a wood a Piggy-wig stood,
   With a ring at the end of his nose,
         His nose,
         His nose,
   With a ring at the end of his nose.

'Dear Pig, are you willing to sell for one shilling
   Your ring?' Said the Piggy, 'I will.'
So they took it away, and were married next day
   By the turkey who lives on the hill.
They dined on mince and slices of quince,
   Which they ate with a runcible spoon;

And hand in hand, on the edge of the sand,
They danced by the light of the moon,
The moon,
The moon,
They danced by the light of the moon.

HOME FROM ABROAD

Far-fetched with tales of other worlds and ways,
My skin well-oiled with wines of the Levant,
I set my face into a filial smile
To greet the pale, domestic kiss of Kent.

But shall I never learn? That gawky girl,
Recalled so primly in my foreign thoughts,
Becomes again the green-haired queen of love
Whose wanton form dilates as it delights.

Her rolling tidal landscape floods the eye
And drowns Chianti in a dusky stream;
The flower-flecked grasses swim with simple horses,
The hedges choke with roses fat as cream.

So do I breathe the hayblown airs of home,
And watch the sea-green elms drip birds and shadows,
And as the twilight nets the plunging sun
My heart's keel slides to rest among the meadows.

Norman MacCaig 1910–

SPARROW

He's no artist:
His taste in clothes is more
dowdy than gaudy.
And his nest – that blackbird, writing
pretty scrolls on the air with the gold nib of his beak,
would call it a slum.

To stalk solitary on lawns,
to sing solitary in midnight trees,
to glide solitary over gray Atlantics –
not for him: he'd rather
a punch-up in a gutter.

He carries what learning he has
lightly – it is, in fact, based only
on the usefulness whose result
is survival. A proletarian bird.
No scholar.

But when winter soft-shoes in
and these other birds –
ballet dancers, musicians, architects –
die in the snow
and freeze to branches,
watch him happily flying
on the O-levels and A-levels
of the air.

Charles Mackay 1814–89

THE SEA-KING'S BURIAL

'My strength is failing fast,'
   Said the Sea-king to his men;–
'I shall never sail the seas
   Like a conqueror again.
But while yet a drop remains
Of the life-blood in my veins,
Raise, oh, raise me from the bed;–
Put the crown upon my head;–
Put my good sword in my hand;
And so lead me to the strand,
Where my ship at anchor rides
             Steadily;
If I cannot end my life
In the bloody battle-strife,
Let me die as I have lived,
          On the sea.'

They have raised King Balder up,
   Put his crown upon his head;
They have sheath'd his limbs in mail,
   And the purple o'er him spread;
And amid the greeting rude
Of a gathering multitude,
Borne him slowly to the shore –
All the energy of yore
From his dim eyes flashing forth –
Old sea-lion of the North; –
As he look'd upon his ship
          Riding free.
And on his forehead pale

Felt the cold refreshing gale,
And heard the welcome sound
                    Of the sea.

They have borne him to the ship
          With a slow and solemn tread;
They have placed him on the deck
          With his crown upon his head,
Where he sat as on a throne;
And have left him there alone,
With his anchor ready weigh'd,
And the snowy sails display'd
To the favouring wind, once more
Blowing freshly from the shore;
And have bidden him farewell
                    Tenderly;
Saying, 'King of mighty men,
We shall meet thee yet again,
In Valhalla, with the monarchs
                    Of the sea.'

Underneath him in the hold
          They had placed the lighted brand;
And the fire was burning slow
          As the vessel from the land,
Like a stag-hound from the slips,
Darted forth from out the ships; –
There was music in her sail
As it swell'd before the gale,
And a dashing at her prow
As it cleft the waves below,
And the good ship sped along,
                    Scudding free.
As on many a battle morn
In her time she had been borne,

To struggle, and to conquer
                    On the sea.

And Balder spake no more,
    And no sound escaped his lip; –
And he look'd, yet scarcely saw
    The destruction of his ship;
Nor the fleet sparks mounting high,
Nor the glare upon the sky; –
Scarcely heard the billows dash,
Nor the burning timber crash; –
Scarcely felt the scorching heat
That was gathering at his feet,
Nor the fierce flames mounting o'er him
                    Greedily.
But the life was in him yet,
And the courage to forget
All his pain, in his triumph
                    On the sea.

Once alone a cry arose,
    Half of anguish, half of pride,
As he sprang upon his feet,
    With the flames on every side.
'I am coming!' said the King,
'Where the swords and bucklers ring –
Where the warrior lives again
With the souls of mighty men –
Where the weary find repose,
And the red wine ever flows; –
I am coming, great All-Father,
                    Unto thee!
Unto Odin, unto Thor,
And the strong true hearts of yore –
I am coming to Valhalla,
                    O'er the sea.'

Red and fierce upon the sky
    Until midnight, shone the glare,
And the burning ship drove on –
    Like a meteor of the air.
She was driven and hurried past,
'Mid the roaring of the blast.
And of Balder, warrior-born,
Naught remain'd at break of morn,
On the charr'd and blacken'd hull,
But some ashes and a skull;
And still the vessel drifted
                    Heavily,
    With a pale a hazy light
    Until far into the night,
When the storm had spent its rage
                    On the sea.

    Then the ocean ceased her strife
        With the wild winds lull'd to rest,
    And a full, round, placid moon
        Shed a halo on her breast;
    And the burning ship still lay
    On the deep sea, far away;
    From her ribs of solid oak,
    Pouring forth the flame and smoke;
    Until, burnt through all her bulk
    To the water's edge, the hulk
Down a thousand fathoms founder'd
                    Suddenly,
    With a low and sullen sound;
    While the billows sang around
Sad requiems for the monarch
                    Of the sea.

D. M. Mackenzie 1876–1944

MACALLISTER DANCES BEFORE THE KING

Clansmen, the peats are burning bright,
    Sit round them in a ring,
And I will tell of that great night
    I danced before the King.

For as a dancer in my youth
    So great was my renown,
The King himself invited me
    To visit London Town.

My brand new presentation kilt
    And oranaments I wore,
As with my skian-dhu I rapped
    Upon the Palace door.

And soon I heard a lord or duke
    Come running down the stair,
Who to the keyhole put his mouth,
    Demanding who was there.

'Open the door,' I sternly cried,
    'As quickly as you can!
Is this the way that you receive
    A Highland gentleman?'

The door was opened; word went round –
    'Macallister is here!'
And at the news the Palace rang
    With one tremendous cheer.

The King was sitting on his throne,
    But down the steps he came;
Immediately the waiting Lord
    Pronounced my magic name.

The lovely ladies of the Court,
    With pearls and jewels decked,
All blushed and trembled as I bowed
    To them with great respect.

Slowly at first, with hands on hips,
    I danced with ease and grace;
Then raised my hands above my head,
    And swifter grew my pace.

At last no human eye could see
    My steps so light and quick,
And from the floor great clouds of dust
    Came rising fast and thick.

The King was greatly moved, and shook
    My hand in friendship true.
'Alas!' he cried, 'although a King,
    I cannot dance like you!'

And then the gracious Queen herself
    Came shyly up to me,
She pinned a medal on my breast
    For everyone to see.

Her whisper I shall not forget,
    Nor how her eyes grew dim –
'Ah, where was *you*, Macallister,
    That day I married *him?*'

APPLE BLOSSOM

The first blossom was the best blossom
For the child who never had seen an orchard;
For the youth whom whisky had led astray
The morning after was the first day.

The first apple was the best apple
For Adam before he heard the sentence;
When the flaming sword endorsed the Fall
The trees were his to plant for all.

The first ocean was the best ocean
For the child from streets of doubt and litter;
For the youth for whom the skies unfurled
His first love was his first world.

But the first verdict seemed the worst verdict
When Adam and Eve were expelled from Eden;
Yet when the bitter gates clanged to
The sky beyond was just as blue.

For the next ocean is the first ocean
And the last ocean is the first ocean
And, however often the sun may rise,
A new thing dawns upon our eyes.

For the last blossom is the first blossom
And the first blossom is the best blossom
And when from Eden we take our way
The morning after is the first day.

SILVER

Slowly, silently, now the moon
Walks the night in her silver shoon;
This way, and that, she peers, and sees
Silver fruit upon silver trees;
One by one the casements catch
Her beams beneath the silvery thatch;
Couched in his kennel, like a log,
With paws of silver sleeps the dog;
From their shadowy cote the white breasts peep
Of doves in a silver-feathered sleep;
A harvest mouse goes scampering by,
With silver claws, and silver eye;
And moveless fish in the water gleam,
By silver reeds in a silver stream.

John Masefield 1878–1967

THE WEST WIND

It's a warm wind, the west wind, full of birds' cries;
I never hear the west wind but tears are in my eyes.
For it comes from the west lands, the old brown hills,
And April's in the west wind, and daffodils.

It's a fine land, the west land, for hearts as tired as mine,
Apple orchards blossom there, and the air's like wine.
There is cool green grass there, where men may lie at rest,
And the thrushes are in song there, fluting from the nest.

'Will ye not come home, brother? ye have been long away,
It's April, and blossom time, and white is the may;
And bright is the sun, brother, and warm is the rain, –
Will ye not come home, brother, home to us again?

'The young corn is green, brother, where the rabbits run,
It's blue sky, and white clouds, and warm rain and sun.
It's song to a man's soul, brother, fire to a man's brain,
To hear the wild bees and see the merry spring again.

'Larks are singing in the west, brother, above the green wheat,
So will ye not come home, brother, and rest your tired feet?
I've a balm for bruised hearts, brother, sleep for aching eyes,'
Says a warm wind, the west wind, full of birds' cries.

It's the white road westwards is the road I must tread
To the green grass, the cool grass, and rest for heart and head,
To the violets and the warm hearts and the thrushes' song,
In the fine land, the west land, the land where I belong.

Roger McGough 1937–

_____

AT LUNCHTIME

When the bus stopped suddenly
to avoid damaging
a mother and child in the road,
the younglady in the green hat sitting opposite,
was thrown across me,
and not being one to miss an opportunity
i started to make love.

At first, she resisted,
saying that it was too early in the morning,
and too soon after breakfast,
and anyway, she found me repulsive.
But when i explained
that this being a nuclearage
the world was going to end at lunchtime,
she took off her green hat,
put her busticket into her pocket
and joined in the exercise.

The buspeople,
and there were many of them,
were shockedandsurprised,
and amusedandannoyed.
But when word got around
that the world was going to end at lunchtime,
they put their pride in their pockets
with their bustickets
and made love one with the other.
And even the busconductor,
feeling left out,

climbed into the cab,
and struck up some sort of relationship with the driver.

That night,
on the bus coming home,
we were all a little embarrassed.
Especially me and the younglady in the green hat.
And we all started to say
in different ways
how hasty and foolish we had been.
But then, always having been a bitofalad,
i stood up and said it was a pity
that the world didnt nearly end every lunchtime,
and that we could always pretend.
And then it happened . . .

Quick asa crash
we all changed partners,
and soon the bus was aquiver
with white, mothball bodies doing naughty things.

And the next day
and everyday
In everybus
In everystreet
In everytown
In everycountry

People pretended
that the world was coming to an end at lunchtime.
It still hasnt.
Although in a way it has.

AFTERNOON TEA

Please you, excuse me, good five-o'clock people,
    I've lost my last hatful of words,
And my heart's in the wood up above the church steeple,
    I'd rather have tea with the birds.

Gay Kate's stolen kisses, poor Barnaby's scars,
    John's losses and Mary's gains,
Oh! what do they matter, my dears, to the stars
    Or the glow-worms in the lanes!

I'd rather lie under the tall elm-trees,
    With old rooks talking loud overhead,
To watch a red squirrel run over my knees,
    Very still on my brackeny bed.

And wonder what feathers the wrens will be taking
    For lining their nests next Spring;
Or why the tossed shadow of boughs in a great wind shaking
    Is such a lovely thing.

THE KING'S BREAKFAST

The King asked
The Queen, and
The Queen asked
The Dairymaid:
'Could we have some butter for
The Royal slice of bread?'
The Queen asked
The Dairymaid,
The Dairymaid
Said, 'Certainly,
I'll go and tell
The cow
Now
Before she goes to bed.'

The Dairymaid
She curtsied,
And went and told
The Alderney:
'Don't forget the butter for
The Royal slice of bread.'
The Alderney
Said sleepily:
'You'd better tell
His Majesty
That many people nowadays
Like marmalade
Instead.'

The Dairymaid
Said, 'Fancy!'
And went to
Her Majesty.
She curtsied to the Queen, and
She turned a little red:
'Excuse me
Your Majesty,
For taking of
The liberty,
But marmalade is tasty, if
It's very
Thickly
Spread.'

The Queen said
'Oh!'
And went to
His Majesty:
'Talking of the butter for
The Royal slice of bread,
Many people
Think that
Marmalade
Is nicer.
Would you like to try a little
Marmalade
Instead?'

The King said,
'Bother!'
And then he said,
'Oh, deary me!'
The King sobbed, 'Oh deary me!'
And went back to bed.

'Nobody,'
He whimpered,
'Could call me
A fussy man;
I *only* want
A little bit
Of butter for
My bread!'

The Queen said
'There, there!'
And went to
The Dairymaid.
The Dairymaid
Said, 'There, there!'
And went to the shed.
The cow said
There, there!
'I didn't really
Mean it;
Here's milk for his porringer
And butter for his bread.'

The Queen took
The butter
And brought it to
His Majesty;
The King said,
'Butter, eh?'
And bounced out of bed.
'Nobody,' he said,
As he kissed her
Tenderly,
Nobody,' he said,
As he slid down

The banisters,
'Nobody,
My darling,
Could call me
A fussy man–
BUT
I do like a little bit of butter to my bread!"

John Milton 1608–74

SONNET XVI: 'WHEN I CONSIDER HOW MY LIGHT IS SPENT'

When I consider how my light is spent,
   E're half my days, in this dark world and wide,
   And that one Talent which is death to hide,
   Lodg'd with me useless, though my Soul more bent
To serve therewith my Maker, and present
   My true account, least he returning chide,
   Doth God exact day-labour, light deny'd,
   I fondly ask; But patience to prevent
That murmur, soon replies, God doth not need
   Either man's work or his own gifts, who best
   Bear his milde yoak, they serve him best, his State
Is Kingly. Thousands at his bidding speed
   And post o're Land and Ocean without rest:
   They also serve who only stand and waite.

CHILD'S SONG IN SPRING

The silver birch is a dainty lady,
    She wears a satin gown;
The elm-tree makes the churchyard shady,
    She will not live in town.

The English oak is a sturdy fellow;
    He gets his green coat late;
The willow is smart in a suit of yellow,
    While brown the beech trees wait.

Such a gay green gown God gives the larches –
    As green as He is good!
The hazels hold up their arms for arches
    When Spring rides through the wood.

The chestnut's proud, and the lilac's pretty,
    The poplar's gentle and tall,
But the plane tree's kind to the poor dull city –
    I love him best of all!

Sir Henry Newbolt 1862–1938

_____

VITAI LAMPADA

There's a breathless hush in the Close to-night –
   Ten to make and the match to win –
A bumping pitch and a blinding light,
   An hour to play and the last man in.
And it's not for the sake of a ribboned coat,
   Or the selfish hope of a season's fame,
But his Captain's hand on his shoulder smote –
   'Play up! play up! and play the game!'

The sand of the desert is sodden red, –
   Red with the wreck of a square that broke; –
The Gatling's jammed and the Colonel dead,
   And the regiment blind with dust and smoke.
The river of death has brimmed his banks,
   And England's far, and Honour a name,
But the voice of a schoolboy rallies the ranks:
   'Play up! play up! and play the game!'

This is the word that year by year,
   While in her place the School is set,
Every one of her sons must hear,
   And none that hears it dare forget.
This they all with a joyful mind
   Bear through life like a torch in flame,
And falling fling to the host behind –
   'Play up! play up! and play the game!'

Lady Caroline Norton 1808–77

I DO NOT LOVE THEE

I do not love thee! – no! I do not love thee!
And yet when thou art absent I am sad;
   And envy even the bright blue sky above thee,
Whose quiet stars may see thee and be glad.

I do not love thee! – yet, I know not why,
Whate'er thou dost seems still well done, to me:
   And often in my solitude I sigh
That those I do love are not more like thee!

I do not love thee! – yet, when thou art gone,
I hate the sound (though those who speak be dear)
   Which breaks the lingering echo of the tone
Thy voice of music leaves upon my ear.

I do not love thee! – yet thy speaking eyes,
With their deep, bright, and most expressive blue,
   Between me and the midnight heaven arise,
Oftener than any eyes I ever knew.

I know I do not love thee! yet, alas!
Others will scarcely trust my candid heart;
   And oft I catch them smiling as they pass,
Because they see me gazing where thou art.

WIZARDRY

There's many a proud wizard in Araby and Egypt
  Can read the silver writing of the stars as they run;
And many a dark gypsy, with a pheasant in his knapsack,
  Has gathered more by moonshine than wiser men have won;

But *I* know a Wizardry
  Can take a buried acorn
And whisper forests out of it, to tower against the sun.

There's many a magician in Bagdad and Benares
  Can read you – for a penny – what your future is to be;
And a flock of crazy prophets that by staring at a crystal
  Can fill it with more fancies than there's herring in the sea;

But *I* know a Wizardry
  Can break a freckled egg-shell
And shake a throstle out of it, in every hawthorn-tree.

There's many a crafty alchemist in Mecca and Jerusalem;
  And Michael Scott and Merlin were reckoned very wise;

But *I* know a Wizardry
  Can take a wisp of sun fire
And round it to a planet and roll it through the skies,
  With cities, and sea-ports, and little shining windows,
And hedgerows and gardens and loving human eyes. . . .

Wilfred Owen 1893–1918

STRANGE MEETING

It seemed that out of battle I escaped
Down some profound dull tunnel, long since scooped
Through granites which titanic wars had groined.
Yet also there encumbered sleepers groaned,
Too fast in thought or death to be bestirred.
Then, as I probed them, one sprang up, and stared
With piteous recognition in fixed eyes,
Lifting distressful hands, as if to bless.
And by his smile, I knew that sullen hall, –
By his dead smile I knew we stood in Hell.
With a thousand pains that vision's face was grained;
Yet no blood reached there from the upper ground,
And no guns thumped, or down the flues made moan.
'Strange friend,' I said, 'here is no cause to mourn.'
'None,' said that other, 'save the undone years,
The hopelessness. Whatever hope is yours,
Was my life also; I went hunting wild
After the wildest beauty in the world,
Which lies not calm in eyes, or braided hair,
But mocks the steady running of the hour,
And if it grieves, grieves richlier than here.
For by my glee might many men have laughed,
And of my weeping something had been left,
Which must die now. I mean the truth untold,
The pity of war, the pity war distilled.
Now men will go content with what we spoiled,
Or, discontent, boil bloody, and be spilled.
They will be swift with swiftness of the tigress.
None will break ranks, though nations trek from progress.

Courage was mine, and I had mystery,
Wisdom was mine, and I had mastery:
To miss the march of this retreating world
Into vain citadels that are not walled.
Then, when much blood had clogged their chariot-wheels,
I would go up and wash them from sweet wells,
Even with truths that lie too deep for taint.
I would have poured my spirit without stint
But not through wounds; not on the cess of war.
Foreheads of men have bled where no wounds were.
I am the enemy you killed, my friend.
I knew you in this dark: for so you frowned
Yesterday through me as you jabbed and killed.
I parried; but my hands were loath and cold.
Let us sleep now. . . .'

Thomas Love Peacock 1785–1866

———————

LOVE AND AGE

I play'd with you 'mid cowslips blowing,
    When I was six and you were four;
When garlands weaving, flower-balls throwing,
    Were pleasures soon to please no more.
Through groves and meads, o'er grass and heather,
    With little playmates, to and fro,
We wander'd hand in hand together;
    But that was sixty years ago.

You grew a lovely roseate maiden,
    And still our early love was strong;
Still with no care our days were laden,
    They glided joyously along;
And I did love you very dearly,
    How dearly words want power to show;
I thought your heart was touch'd as nearly;
    But that was fifty years ago.

Then other lovers came around you,
    Your beauty grew from year to year,
And many a splendid circle found you
    The centre of its glittering sphere.
I saw you then, first vows forsaking,
    On rank and wealth your hand bestow;
O, then I thought my heart was breaking! –
    But that was forty years ago.

And I lived on, to wed another:
    No cause she gave me to repine;
And when I heard you were a mother,
    I did not wish the children mine.

My own young flock, in fair progression,
    Made up a pleasant Christmas row:
My joy in them was past expression;
    But that was thirty years ago.

You grew a matron plump and comely,
    You dwelt in fashion's brightest blaze;
My earthly lot was far more homely;
    But I too had my festal days.
No merrier eyes have ever glisten'd
    Around the hearth-stone's wintry glow,
Than when my youngest child was christen'd;
    But that was twenty years ago.

Time pass'd. My eldest girl was married,
    And I am now a grandsire gray;
One pet of four years old I've carried
    Among the wild-flower'd meads to play.
In our old fields of childish pleasure,
    Where now, as then, the cowslips blow,
She fills her basket's ample measure;
    And that is not ten years ago.

But though first love's impassion'd blindness
    Has pass'd away in colder light,
I still have thought of you with kindness,
    And shall do, till our last good-night.
That ever-rolling silent hours
    Will bring a time we shall not know,
When our young days of gathering flowers
    Will be an hundred years ago.

Mervyn Peake 1911–68

THE COCKY WALKERS

Grouped nightly at the cold, accepted wall,
Carved with a gaslight chisel the lean heads
Cry out unwittingly for Rembrandt's needle.
These are the flashy saplings whose domain
I cannot enter.
They burn at lip and fingertips the stuffed paper;
The trouser-pocket boys, the cocky walkers,
Sons of old mothers, with their hats askew
Hummock the shoulder to the little flower
That lights the palm into a nightmare land,
A bloody basin of the sterile moon
That lights the face that sprouts the cigarette
Into a sudden passion of fierce colour.
Down the cold corridor of winter nights
I see a thousand groups that keep
The fag alight, at walls, and in the sharp
Stern corners of the street:
These are the sprigs; flash boys, uncaught,
Treading the reedy springboard of green days.
Theirs is a headiness, for they
Have burned their lives up to the quarter-mark.
The days move by them and the chill nights hold them
In an old, unthought conspiracy, for they
Tinkle upon tin feet that send no root.
I see them at the cold, accepted wall,
The trouser-pocket boys, the cocky walkers.

ANNABEL LEE

It was many and many a year ago,
    In a kingdom by the sea,
That a maiden there lived whom you may know
    By the name of ANNABEL LEE;
And this maiden she lived with no other thought
    Than to love and be loved by me.

I was a child and *she* was a child,
    In this kingdom by the sea:
But we loved with a love that was more than love –
    I and my ANNABEL LEE;
With a love that the winged seraphs of heaven
    Coveted her and me.

And this was the reason that, long ago,
    In this kingdom by the sea,
A wind blew out of a cloud, chilling
    My beautiful ANNABEL LEE;
So that her highborn kinsmen came
    And bore her away from me,
To shut her up in a sepulchre
    In this kingdom by the sea.

The angels, not half so happy in heaven,
    Went envying her and me –
Yes! – that was the reason (as all men know,
    In this kingdom by the sea)
That the wind came out of the cloud by night,
    Chilling and killing my ANNABEL LEE.

But our love it was stronger by far than the love
  Of those who were older than we –
  Of many far wiser than we –
And neither the angels in heaven above,
  Nor the demons down under the sea,
Can ever dissever my soul from the soul
  Of the beautiful ANNABEL LEE!

For the moon never beams, without bringing me dreams
  Of the beautiful ANNABEL LEE;
And the stars never rise, but I feel the bright eyes
  Of the beautiful ANNABEL LEE;
And so, all the night-tide, I lie down by the side
Of my darling, – my darling, – my life and my bride,
  In her sepulchre there by the sea,
  In her tomb by the side of the sea.

Alexander Pope 1688–1744

THE DYING CHRISTIAN TO HIS SOUL
ODE

I

Vital spark of heavenly flame!
Quit, oh quit this mortal frame!
Trembling, hoping, lingering, flying,
Oh the pain, the bliss of dying!
Cease, fond Nature, cease thy strife,
And let me languish into life!

II

Hark! they whisper; angels say,
'Sister Spirit, come away!'
What is this absorbs me quite?
Steals my senses, shuts my sight,
Drowns my spirits, draws my breath?
Tell me, my Soul, can this be death?

III

The world recedes; it disappears!
Heaven opens on my eyes! my ears
      With sounds seraphic ring:
Lend, lend your wings! I mount! I fly!
O Grave! where is thy victory?
      O Death! where is thy sting?

THE PASSIONATE MAN'S PILGRIMAGE

Give me my scallop shell of quiet,
My staff of faith to walk upon,
My scrip of joy, immortal diet,
My bottle of salvation:
My gown of glory, hope's true gage,
And thus I'll take my pilgrimage.

Blood must be my body's balmer,
No other balm shall there be given,
Whilst my soul, like a white palmer,
Travels to the land of heaven,
Over the silver mountains,
Where spring the nectar fountains:
And there I'll kiss
The bowl of bliss,
And drink my eternal fill
On every milken hill,
My soul will be a-dry before,
But after, it will ne'er thirst more.

And by the happy blissful way
More peaceful pilgrims I shall see,
That have shook off their gowns of clay,
And go apparelled fresh like me.
I'll bring them first
To slake their thirst,
And then to taste those nectar suckets
At the clear wells
Where sweetness dwells,
Drawn up by saints in crystal buckets.

And when our bottles and all we
Are filled with immortality:
Then the holy paths we'll travel
Strewed with rubies thick as gravel,
Ceilings of diamonds, sapphire floors,
High walls of coral and pearl bowers.

From thence to heaven's bribeless hall
Where no corrupted voices brawl,
No conscience molten into gold,
No forged accusers bought and sold,
No cause deferred, no vain spent journey,
For there Christ is the King's Attorney:
Who pleads for all without degrees,
And he hath Angels, but no fees.

When the grand twelve million jury,
Of our sins with sinful fury,
'Gainst our souls black verdicts give,
Christ pleads his death, and then we live,
Be thou my speaker, taintless pleader,
Unblotted lawyer, true proceeder,
Thou movest salvation even for alms:
Not with a bribèd lawyer's palms.

And this is my eternal plea,
To him that made Heaven, Earth and Sea,
Seeing my flesh must die so soon,
And want a head to dine next noon,
Just at the stroke when my veins start and spread,
Set on my soul an everlasting head,
Then am I ready like a palmer fit,
To tread those blest paths which before I writ.

Irina Ratushinskaya 1954–

I WILL LIVE AND SURVIVE
Translated by David McDuff

I will live and survive and be asked:
How they slammed my head against a trestle,
How I had to freeze at nights,
How my hair started to turn grey . . .
But I'll smile. And will crack some joke
And brush away the encroaching shadow.
And I will render homage to the dry September
That became my second birth.
And I'll be asked: 'Doesn't it hurt you to remember?'
Not being deceived by my outward flippancy.
But the former names will detonate in my memory –
Magnificent as old cannon.
And I will tell of the best people in all the earth,
The most tender, but also the most invincible,
How they said farewell, how they went to be tortured,
How they waited for letters from their loved ones.
And I'll be asked: what helped us to live
When there were neither letters nor any news – only walls,
And the cold of the cell, and the blather of official lies,
And the sickening promises made in exchange for betrayal.
And I will tell of the first beauty
I saw in captivity.
A frost-covered window! No spyholes, nor walls,
Nor cell-bars, nor the long-endured pain –
Only a blue radiance on a tiny pane of glass,
A cast pattern – none more beautiful could be dreamt!
The more clearly you looked, the more powerfully blossomed
Those brigand forests, campfires and birds!
And how many times there was bitter cold weather

And how many windows sparkled after that one –
But never was it repeated,
That upheaval of rainbow ice!
And anyway, what good would it be to me now,
And what would be the pretext for that festival?
Such a gift can only be received once,
And perhaps is only needed once.

J. W. Riley 1849–1916

_____

WHEN THE FROST IS ON THE PUNKIN

When the frost is on the punkin and the fodder's in the
    shock,
And you hear the kyouck and gobble of the struttin' turkey-
    cock,
And the clackin' of the guineys, and the cluckin' of the hens,
And the rooster's hallylooer as he tiptoes on the fence;
O, it's then's the times a feller is a-feelin' at his best,
With the risin' sun to greet him from a night of peaceful rest,
As he leaves the house, bareheaded, and goes out to feed the
    stock,
When the frost is on the punkin and the fodder's in the
    shock.

They's something kindo' harty-like about the atmusfere
When the heat of summer's over and the coolin' fall is here –
Of course we miss the flowers, and the blossums on the trees,
And the mumble of the hummin'-birds and buzzin' of the
    bees;
But the air's so appetizin'; and the landscape through the haze
Of a crisp and sunny morning of the airly autumn days
Is a pictur' that no painter has the colorin' to mock –
When the frost is on the punkin and the fodder's in the
    shock.

The husky, rusty russel of the tossels of the corn,
And the raspin' of the tangled leaves, as golden as the morn;
The stubble in the furries – kindo' lonesome-like, but still
A-preachin' sermons to us of the barns they growed to fill;
The strawstack in the medder, and the reaper in the shed;
The hosses in theyr stalls below – the clover overhead! –

O, it sets my hart a-clickin' like the tickin' of a clock,
When the frost is on the punkin and the fodder's in the
    shock!

Then your apples all is gethered, and the ones a feller keeps
Is poured around the celler-floor in red and yeller heaps;
And your cider-makin' 's over, and your wimmern-folks is
    through
With their mince and apple-butter, and theyr souse and
    sausage, too! . . .
I don't know how to tell it – but ef sich a thing could be
As the Angels wantin' boardin', and they'd call around on
    me –
I'd want to 'commodate 'em – all the whole-indurin' flock –
When the frost is on the punkin and the fodder's in the
    shock!

REMEMBER

Remember me when I am gone away,
    Gone far away into the silent land;
When you can no more hold me by the hand,
Nor I half turn to go yet turning stay.
Remember me when no more day by day
    You tell me of our future that you planned:
    Only remember me; you understand
It will be late to counsel then or pray.
Yet if you should forget me for a while
    And afterwards remember, do not grieve:
    For if the darkness and corruption leave
    A vestige of the thoughts that once I had,
Better by far you should forget and smile
    Than that you should remember and be sad.

Vita Sackville-West 1892–1962

THE GREATER CATS

The greater cats with golden eyes
Stare out between the bars.
Deserts are there, and different skies,
And night with different stars.
They prowl the aromatic hill,
And mate as fiercely as they kill,
And hold the freedom of their will
To roam, to live, to drink their fill;
But this beyond their wit know I:
Man loves a little, and for long shall die.

Their kind across the desert range
Where tulips spring from stones,
Not knowing they will suffer change
Or vultures pick their bones.
Their strength's eternal in their sight,
They rule the terror of the night,
They overtake the deer in flight,
And in their arrogance they smite;
But I am sage, if they are strong:
Man's love is transient as his death is long.

Yet oh what powers to deceive!
My wit is turned to faith,
And at this moment I believe
In love, and scout at death.
I came from nowhere, and shall be
Strong, steadfast, swift, eternally:
I am a lion, a stone, a tree,

And as the Polar star in me
Is fixed my constant heart on thee.
Ah, may I stay forever blind
With lions, tigers, leopards, and their kind.

SECRET MUSIC

I keep such music in my brain
No din this side of death can quell;
Glory exulting over pain,
And beauty, garlanded in hell.

My dreaming spirit will not heed
The roar of guns that would destroy
My life that on the gloom can read
Proud-surging melodies of joy.

To the world's end I went, and found
Death in his carnival of glare;
But in my torment I was crowned,
And music dawned above despair.

Vernon Scannell 1922–

_____

AFTER THE FIREWORKS

Back into the light and warmth,
Boots clogged with mud, toes
Welded to wedges of cold flesh,
The children warm their hands on mugs
While, on remembered lawns, the flash
Of fireworks dazzles night;
Sparklers spray and rockets swish,
Soar high and break in falling showers
Of glitter; the bonfire gallivants,
Its lavish flames shimmy, prance,
And lick the straddling guy.
We wait for those great leaves of heat
And broken necklaces of light
To dim and die.
And then the children go to bed.
Tomorrow they will search grey ground
For debris of tonight: the sad
And saturated cardboard stems,
The fallen rocket sticks, the charred
Hubs of catherine-wheels;
Then, having gathered all they've found,
They'll leave them scattered carelessly
For us to clear away.
But now the children are asleep,
And you and I sit silently
And hear, from far off in the night,
The last brave rocket burst and fade.
We taste the darkness in the light,
Reflect that fireworks are not cheap
And ask ourselves uneasily
If, even now, we've fully paid.

LOCHINVAR

O, young Lochinvar is come out of the west,
Through all the wide Border his steed was the best;
And save his good broadsword he weapons had none,
He rode all unarmed, and he rode all alone.
So faithful in love, and so dauntless in war,
There never was knight like the young Lochinvar.

He staid not for brake, and he stopped not for stone.
He swam the Eske river where ford there was none;
But ere he alighted at Netherby gate,
The bride had consented, the gallant came late:
For a laggard in love, and a dastard in war,
Was to wed the fair Ellen of brave Lochinvar.

So boldly he entered the Netherby Hall,
Among bride's-men, and kinsmen, and brothers, and all:
Then spoke the bride's father, his hand on his sword,
(For the poor craven bridegroom said never a word,)
'O come ye in peace here, or come ye in war,
Or to dance at our bridal, young Lord Lochinvar?'

'I long wooed your daughter, my suit you denied; –
Love swells like the Solway, but ebbs like its tide –
And now am I come, with this lost love of mine,
To lead but one measure, drink one cup of wine.
There are maidens in Scotland more lovely by far,
That would gladly be bride to the young Lochinvar.'

The bride kissed the goblet: the knight took it up,
He quaffed off the wine, and he threw down the cup.

She looked down to blush, and she looked up to sigh,
With a smile on her lips, and a tear in her eye.
He took her soft hand, ere her mother could bar, –
'Now tread we a measure!' said young Lochinvar.

So stately his form, and so lovely her face,
That never a hall such a galliard did grace;
While her mother did fret, and her father did fume.
And the bridegroom stood dangling his bonnet and plume;
And the bride-maidens whispered "Twere better by far,
To have matched our fair cousin with young Lochinvar.'

One touch to her hand, and one word in her ear,
When they reached the hall-door, and the charger stood near;
So light to the croupe the fair lady he swung,
So light to the saddle before her he sprung!
'She is won! we are gone, over bank, bush, and scaur;
They'll have fleet steeds that follow,' quoth young Lochinvar.

There was mounting 'mong Græmes of the Netherby clan;
Forsters, Fenwicks, and Musgraves, they rode and they ran:
There was racing and chasing on Cannobie Lee,
But the lost bride of Netherby ne'er did they see.
So daring in love, and so dauntless in war,
Have ye e'er heard of gallant like young Lochinvar? –

William Shakespeare 1564–1616

SONNET CXVI: LET ME NOT TO
THE MARRIAGE OF TRUE MINDS

Let me not to the marriage of true minds
Admit impediments. Love is not love
Which alters when it alteration finds,
Or bends with the remover to remove:
O, no! it is an ever-fixed mark,
That looks on tempests and is never shaken;
It is the star to every wandering bark,
Whose worth's unknown, although his height be taken.
Love's not Time's fool, though rosy lips and cheeks
Within his bending sickle's compass come;
Love alters not with his brief hours and weeks,
But bears it out even to the edge of doom.
    If this be error, and upon me prov'd,
    I never writ, nor no man ever lov'd.

THE CLOUD

I bring fresh showers for the thirsting flowers,
    From the seas and the streams;
I bear light shade for the leaves when laid
    In their noonday dreams.
From my wings are shaken the dews that waken
    The sweet buds every one,
When rocked to rest on their mother's breast,
    As she dances about the sun.
I wield the flail of the lashing hail,
    And whiten the green plains under,
And then again I dissolve it in rain,
    And laugh as I pass in thunder.

I sift the snow on the mountains below,
    And their great pines groan aghast;
And all the night 'tis my pillow white,
    While I sleep in the arms of the blast.
Sublime on the towers of my skiey bowers,
    Lightning my pilot sits;
In a cavern under is fettered the thunder,
    It struggles and howls at fits;
Over earth and ocean, with gentle motion,
    This pilot is guiding me,
Lured by the love of the genii that move
    In the depths of the purple sea;
Over the rills, and the crags, and the hills,
    Over the lakes and the plains,
Wherever he dream, under mountain or stream,
    The Spirit he loves remains;
And I all the while bask in Heaven's blue smile,
    Whilst he is dissolving in rains.

The sanguine Sunrise, with his meteor eyes,
    And his burning plumes outspread,
Leaps on the back of my sailing rack,
    When the morning star shines dead;
As on the jag of a mountain crag,
    Which an earthquake rocks and swings,
An eagle alit one moment may sit
    In the light of its golden wings.
And when Sunset may breathe, from the lit sea beneath,
    Its ardours of rest and of love,
And the crimson pall of eve may fall
    From the depth of Heaven above,
With wings folded I rest, on mine aëry nest,
    As still as a brooding dove.

That orbèd maiden with white fire laden,
    Whom mortals call the Moon,
Glides glimmering o'er my fleece-like floor,
    By the midnight breezes strewn;
And wherever the beat of her unseen feet,
    Which only the angels hear,
May have broken the woof of my tent's thin roof,
    The stars peep behind her and peer;
And I laugh to see them whirl and flee,
    Like a swarm of golden bees,
When I widen the rent in my wind-built tent,
    Till the calm rivers, lakes, and seas,
Like strips of the sky fallen through me on high,
    Are each paved with the moon and these.

I bind the Sun's throne with a burning zone,
    And the Moon's with a girdle of pearl;
The volcanoes are dim, and the stars reel and swim,
    When the whirlwinds my banner unfurl.
From cape to cape, with a bridge-like shape,
    Over a torrent sea,

Sunbeam-proof, I hang like a roof, –
　　The mountains its columns be.
The triumphal arch through which I march
　　With hurricane, fire, and snow,
When the Powers of the air are chained to my chair,
　　Is the million-coloured bow;
The sphere-fire above its soft colours wove,
　　While the moist Earth was laughing below.

I am the daughter of Earth and Water,
　　And the nursling of the Sky;
I pass through the pores of the ocean and shores;
　　I change, but I cannot die.
For after the rain when with never a stain
　　The pavilion of Heaven is bare,
And the winds and sunbeams with their convex gleams
　　Build up the blue dome of air,
I silently laugh at my own cenotaph,
　　And out of the caverns of rain,
Like a child from the womb, like a ghost from the tomb,
　　I arise and unbuild it again.

_____

NEVERTHELESS

Nevertheless
  Nevertheless
    The bird
     Sings
Never the less

Though the blood
  Though the blood
    Is hurled
     Spills
In a hundred
  In a thousand
    Streets of the murdering world.

Nevertheless
  Nevertheless
    The grass
     Springs
Never the less

Though the stones
  Though the stones
    Block
All the hills
  All the plains
    Fields of the inimical world.

Nevertheless
   Nevertheless
      The word
         Rings
         Fills
All the dumb and tongueless spaces of the world

For nevertheless
   Nevertheless
      Love;
Though the fire
      Falls
On all the landlocked lovers in the world

Who nevertheless
   Nevertheless
      Love;
Never,
   Never the less,
      Love

THE SINGING CAT

It was a little captive cat
    Upon a crowded train
His mistress takes him from his box
    To ease his fretful pain.

She holds him tight upon her knee
    The graceful animal
And all the people look at him
    He is so beautiful.

But oh he pricks and oh he prods
    And turns upon her knee
Then lifteth up his innocent voice
    In plaintive melody.

He lifteth up his innocent voice
    He lifteth up, he singeth
And to each human countenance
    A smile of grace he bringeth.

He lifteth up his innocent paw
    Upon her breast he clingeth
And everybody cries, Behold
    The cat, the cat that singeth.

He lifteth up his innocent voice
    He lifteth up, he singeth
And all the people warm themselves
    In the love his beauty bringeth.

Sir Stephen Spender 1909–

THE TRULY GREAT

I think continually of those who were truly great.
Who, from the womb, remembered the soul's history
Through corridors of light, where the hours are suns,
Endless and singing. Whose lovely ambition
Was that their lips, still touched with fire,
Should tell of the Spirit, clothed from head to foot in song.
And who hoarded from the Spring branches
The desires falling across their bodies like blossoms.

What is precious, is never to forget
The essential delight of the blood drawn from ageless springs
Breaking through rocks in worlds before our earth.
Never to deny its pleasure in the morning simple light
Nor its grave evening demand for love.
Never to allow gradually the traffic to smother
With noise and fog, the flowering of the spirit.

Near the snow, near the sun, in the highest fields,
See how these names are fêted by the waving grass
And by the streamers of white cloud
And whispers of wind in the listening sky.
The names of those who in their lives fought for life,
Who wore at their hearts the fire's centre.
Born of the sun, they travelled a short while toward the sun
And left the vivid air signed with their honour.

IN THE POPPY FIELD

Mad Patsy said, he said to me,
That every morning he could see
An angel walking on the sky;
Across the sunny skies of morn
He threw great handfuls far and nigh
Of poppy seed among the corn;
– And then, said he, the angels run
To see the poppies in the sun –

– A poppy is a devil weed, –
I said to him – he disagreed:
He said the devil had no hand
In spreading flowers tall and fair
By corn and rye and meadow land,
And gurth and barrow everywhere:
The devil has not any flower,
But only money in his power.

And then he stretched out in the sun,
And rolled upon his back for fun!
He kicked his legs and roared for joy
Because the sun was shining down!
He said he was a little boy
And wouldn't work for any clown!
He ran and laughed behind a bee;
And danced for very ecstasy!

CHRISTMAS AT SEA

The sheets were frozen hard, and they cut the naked hand;
The decks were like a slide, where a seaman scarce could
    stand;
The wind was a nor'wester, blowing squally off the sea;
And cliffs and spouting breakers were the only thing a-lee.

They heard the surf a-roaring before the break of day;
But 'twas only with the peep of light we saw how ill we lay.
We tumbled every hand on deck instanter, with a shout,
And we gave her the maintops'l, and stood by to go about.
All day we tacked and tacked between the South Head and
    the North;
All day we hauled the frozen sheets, and got no further forth;
All day as cold as charity, in bitter pain and dread,
For very life and nature we tacked from head to head.

We gave the South a wider berth, for there the tide-race
    roared;
But every tack we made we brought the North Head close
    aboard:
So 's we saw the cliffs and houses, and the breakers running
    high,
And the coastguard in his garden, with his glass against his
    eye.

The frost was on the village roofs as white as ocean foam;
The good red fires were burning bright in every 'longshore
    home;
The windows sparkled clear, and the chimneys volleyed out;
And I vow we sniffed the victuals as the vessel went about.

The bells upon the church were rung with a mighty jovial
    cheer;
For it's just that I should tell you how (of all days in the year)
This day of our adversity was blessèd Christmas morn,
And the house above the coastguard's was the house where
      I was born.

O well I saw the pleasant room, the pleasant faces there,
My mother's silver spectacles, my father's silver hair;
And well I saw the firelight, like a flight of homely elves,
Go dancing round the china-plates that stand upon the
    shelves.

And well I knew the talk they had, the talk that was of me,
Of the shadow on the household and the son that went to sea;
And O the wicked fool I seemed, in every kind of way,
To be here and hauling frozen ropes on blessèd Christmas Day.

They lit the high sea-light, and the dark began to fall.
'All hands to loose topgallant sails,' I heard the captain call.
'By the Lord, she'll never stand it,' our first mate, Jackson,
    cried.
. . . 'It's the one way or the other, Mr Jackson,' he replied.

She staggered to her bearings, but the sails were new and good,
And the ship smelt up to windward just as though she
    understood.
As the winter's day was ending, in the entry of the night,
We cleared the weary headland, and passed below the light.

And they heaved a mighty breath, every soul on board but me,
As they saw her nose again pointing handsome out to sea;
But all that I could think of, in the darkness and the cold,
Was just that I was leaving home and my folks were growing
    old.

A. C. Swinburne 1837–1909

_____

A FORSAKEN GARDEN

In a coign of the cliff between lowland and highland,
    At the sea-down's edge between windward and lee,
Walled round with rocks as an inland island,
    The ghost of a garden fronts the sea.
A girdle of brushwood and thorn encloses
    The steep square slope of the blossomless bed
Where the weeds that grew green from the graves of its roses
        Now lie dead.

The fields fall southward, abrupt and broken,
    To the low last edge of the long lone land.
If a step should sound or a word be spoken,
    Would a ghost not rise at the strange guest's hand?
So long have the grey bare walks lain guestless,
    Through branches and briars if a man make way,
He shall find no life but the sea-wind's, restless
        Night and day.

The dense hard passage is blind and stifled
    That crawls by a track none turn to climb
To the strait waste place that the years have rifled
    Of all but the thorns that are touched not of time.
The thorns he spares when the rose is taken;
    The rocks are left when he wastes the plain.
The wind that wanders, the weeds wind-shaken,
        These remain.

Not a flower to be pressed of the foot that falls not;
    As the heart of a dead man the seed-plots are dry;
From the thicket of thorns whence the nightingale calls not,
    Could she call, there were never a rose to reply

Over the meadows that blossom and wither
        Rings but the note of a sea-bird's song;
Only the sun and the rain come hither
        All year long.

The sun burns sere and the rain dishevels
        Only gaunt bleak blossom of scentless breath.
Only the wind here hovers and revels
        In a round where life seems barren as death.
Here there was laughing of old, there was weeping,
        Haply, of lovers none ever will know,
Whose eyes went seaward a hundred sleeping
        Years ago.

Heart handfast in heart as they stood, 'Look thither,'
        Did he whisper? 'look forth from the flowers to the sea;
For the foam-flowers endure when the rose-blossoms wither,
        And men that love lightly may die – but we?'
And the same wind sang and the same waves whitened,
        And or ever the garden's last petals were shed,
In the lips that had whispered, the eyes that had lightened,
        Love was dead.

Or they loved their life through, and then went whither?
        And were one to the end – but what end who knows?
Love deep as the sea as a rose must wither,
        As the rose-red seaweed that mocks the rose.
Shall the dead take thought for the dead to love them?
        What love was ever as deep as a grave?
They are loveless now as the grass above them
        Or the wave.

All are at one now, roses and lovers,
        Not known of the cliffs and the fields and the sea.
Not a breath of the time that has been hovers
        In the air now soft with a summer to be.

Not a breath shall there sweeten the seasons hereafter
    Of the flowers or the lovers that laugh now or weep,
When as they that are free now of weeping and laughter
      We shall sleep.

Here death may deal not again for ever;
    Here change may come not till all change end.
From the graves they have made they shall rise up never,
    Who have left nought living to ravage and rend.
Earth, stones, and thorns of the wild ground growing,
    While the sun and the rain live, these shall be;
Till a last wind's breath upon all these blowing
      Rolls the sea.

Till the slow sea rise and the sheer cliff crumble,
    Till terrace and meadow the deep gulfs drink
Till the strength of the waves of the high tides humble
    The fields that lessen, the rocks that shrink,
Here now in his triumph where all things falter,
    Stretched out on the spoils that his own hand spread,
As a god self-slain on his own strange altar,
      Death lies dead.

Alfred, Lord Tennyson 1809–92

THE LADY OF SHALOTT

PART I

On either side the river lie
Long fields of barley and of rye,
That clothe the wold and meet the sky;
And thro' the field the road runs by
       To many-towered Camelot;
And up and down the people go,
Gazing where the lilies blow
Round an island there below,
       The island of Shalott.

Willows whiten, aspens quiver,
Little breezes dusk and shiver
Thro' the wave that runs for ever
By the island in the river
       Flowing down to Camelot.
Four grey walls, and four grey towers,
Overlook a space of flowers,
And the silent isle imbowers
       The Lady of Shalott.

By the margin, willow-veiled,
Slide the heavy barges trailed
By slow horses; and unhailed
The shallop flitteth silken-sailed
       Skimming down to Camelot:
But who hath seen her wave her hand?
Or at the casement seen her stand?
Or is she known in all the land,
       The Lady of Shalott?

Only reapers, reaping early
In among the bearded barley,
Hear a song that echoes cheerly
From the river winding clearly,
   Down to towered Camelot:
And by the moon the reaper weary,
Piling sheaves in uplands airy,
Listening, whispers "Tis the fairy
   Lady of Shalott.'

PART II

There she weaves by night and day
A magic web with colours gay.
She has heard a whisper say,
A curse is on her if she stay
   To look down to Camelot.
She knows not what the curse may be,
And so she weaveth steadily,
And little other care hath she,
   The Lady of Shalott.

And moving thro' a mirror clear
That hangs before her all the year,
Shadows of the world appear.
There she sees the highway near
   Winding down to Camelot:
There the river eddy whirls,
And there the surly village-churls,
And the red cloaks of market girls,
   Pass onward from Shalott.

Sometimes a troop of damsels glad,
An abbot on an ambling pad,
Sometimes a curly shepherd lad,

Or long-haired page in crimson clad,
Goes by to towered Camelot;
And sometimes thro' the mirror blue
The knights come riding two and two:
She hath no loyal knight and true,
The Lady of Shalott.

But in her web she still delights
To weave the mirror's magic sights,
For often thro' the silent nights
A funeral, with plumes and lights,
And music, went to Camelot:
Or when the moon was overhead,
Came two young lovers lately wed:
'I am half sick of shadows,' said
The Lady of Shalott.

PART III

A bow-shot from her bower-eaves,
He rode between the barley-sheaves,
The sun came dazzling thro' the leaves,
And flamed upon the brazen greaves
Of bold Sir Lancelot.
A red-cross knight for ever kneeled
To a lady in his shield,
That sparkled on the yellow field,
Beside remote Shalott.

The gemmy bridle glittered free,
Like to some branch of stars we see
Hung in the golden Galaxy.
The bridle bells rang merrily
As he rode down to Camelot:
And from his blazoned baldric slung

163

A mighty silver bugle hung,
And as he rode his armour rung,
       Beside remote Shalott.

All in the blue unclouded weather
Thick-jewelled shone the saddle-leather,
The helmet and the helmet-feather
Burned like one burning flame together,
       As he rode down to Camelot.
As often thro' the purple night,
Below the starry clusters bright,
Some bearded meteor, trailing light,
       Moves over still Shalott.

His broad clear brow in sunlight glowed;
On burnished hooves his war-horse trode;
From underneath his helmet flowed
His coal-black curls as on her rode,
       As he rode down to Camelot.
From the bank and from the river
He flashed into the crystal mirror,
'Tirra lirra,' by the river
       Sang Sir Lancelot.

She left the web, she left the loom,
She made three paces thro' the room,
She saw the water-lily bloom,
She saw the helmet and the plume,
       She looked down to Camelot.
Out flew the web and floated wide;
The mirror cracked from side to side;
'The curse is come upon me,' cried
       The Lady of Shalott.

PART IV

In the stormy east-wind straining,
The pale yellow woods were waning,
The broad stream in his banks complaining,
Heavily the low sky raining
      Over towered Camelot;
Down she came and found a boat
Beneath a willow left afloat,
And round about the prow she wrote
      The Lady of Shalott.

And down the river's dim expanse –
Like some bold seër in a trance,
Seeing all his own mischance –
With a glassy countenance
      Did she look to Camelot.
And at the closing of the day
She loosed the chain, and down she lay;
The broad stream bore her far away,
      The Lady of Shalott.

Lying, robed in snowy white
That loosely flew to left and right –
That leaves upon her falling light –
Thro' the noises of the night
      She floated down to Camelot:
And as the boat-head wound along
The willow hills and fields among,
They heard her singing her last song,
      The Lady of Shalott.

Heard a carol, mournful, holy,
Chanted loudly, chanted lowly,
Till her blood was frozen slowly,
And her eyes were darkened wholly,

         Turned to towered Camelot.
For ere she reached upon the tide
The first house by the water-side,
Singing in her song she died,
         The Lady of Shalott.

Under tower and balcony,
By garden wall and gallery,
A gleaming shape she floated by,
Dead-pale between the houses high,
         Silent into Camelot.
Out upon the wharfs they came,
Knight and burgher, lord and dame,
And round the prow they read her name,
         The Lady of Shalott.

Who is this? and what is here?
And in the lighted palace near
Died the sound of royal cheer;
And they crossed themselves for fear,
         All the knights at Camelot:
But Lancelot mused a little space;
He said, 'She has a lovely face;
God in his mercy lend her grace,
         The Lady of Shalott.'

A. S. J. Tessimond 1902–62

CATS

Cats, no less liquid than their shadows,
offer no angles to the wind.
They slip, diminished, neat, through loopholes
Less than themselves; will not be pinned

To rules or routes for journeys; counter
Attack with non-resistance; twist
Enticing through the curving fingers
And leave an angered, empty fist.

They wait, obsequious as darkness,
Quick to retire, quick to return;
Admit no aims or ethics; flatter
With reservations; will not learn

To answer to their names; are seldom
Truly owned till shot and skinned.
Cats, no less liquid than their shadows,
Offer no angles to the wind.

Dylan Thomas 1914–53

—————

THE FORCE THAT THROUGH THE GREEN FUSE DRIVES THE FLOWER

The force that through the green fuse drives the flower
Drives my green age; that blasts the roots of trees
Is my destroyer.
And I am dumb to tell the crooked rose
My youth is bent by the same wintry fever.

The force that drives the water through the rocks
Drives my red blood; that dries the mouthing streams
Turns mine to wax.
And I am dumb to mouth unto my veins
How at the mountain spring the same mouth sucks.

The hand that whirls the water in the pool
Stirs the quicksand; that ropes the blowing wind
Hauls my shroud sail.
And I am dumb to tell the hanging man
How of my clay is made the hangman's lime.

The lips of time leech to the fountain head;
Love drips and gathers, but the fallen blood
Shall calm her sores.
And I am dumb to tell a weather's wind
How time has ticked a heaven round the stars.

And I am dumb to tell my lover's tomb
How at my sheet goes the same crooked worm.

OLD MAN

Old Man, or Lad's love, – in the name there's nothing
To one that knows not Lad's-love, or Old Man,
The hoar-green feathery herb, almost a tree,
Growing with rosemary and lavender.
Even to one that knows it well, the names
Half decorate, half perplex, the thing it is:
At least, what that is clings not to the names
In spite of time. And yet I like the names.

The herb itself I like not, but for certain
I love it, as some day the child will love it
Who plucks a feather from the door-side bush
Whenever she goes in or out of the house.
Often she waits there, snipping the tips and shrivelling
The shreds at last on to the path, perhaps
Thinking, perhaps of nothing, till she sniffs
Her fingers and runs off. The bush is still
But half as tall as she, though it is as old;
So well she clips it. Not a word she says;
And I can only wonder how much hereafter
She will remember, with that bitter scent,
Of garden rows, and ancient damson-trees
Topping a hedge, a bent path to a door,
A low thick bush beside the door, and me
Forbidding her to pick.

        As for myself,
Where first I met the bitter scent is lost.
I, too, often shrivel the grey shreds,
Sniff them and think and sniff again and try

Once more to think what it is I am remembering,
Always in vain, I cannot like the scent,
Yet I would rather give up others more sweet,
With no meaning, than this bitter one.

I have mislaid the key. I sniff the spray
And think of nothing; I see and I hear nothing;
Yet seem, too, to be listening, lying in wait
For what I should, yet never can, remember:
No garden appears, no path, no hoar-green bush
Of Lad's-love, or Old Man, no child beside,
Neither father nor mother, nor any playmate;
Only an avenue, dark, nameless, without end.

TO A SNOWFLAKE

What heart could have thought you? –
Past our devisal
(O filigree petal!)
Fashioned so purely,
Fragilely, surely,
From what Paradisal
Imagineless metal,
Too costly for cost?
Who hammered you, wrought you,
From argentine vapour? –
'God was my shaper.
Passing surmisal,
He hammered, He wrought me,
From curled silver vapour,
To lust of His mind: –
Thou could'st not have thought me!
So purely, so palely,
Tinily, surely,
Mightily, frailly,
Insculped and embossed,
With His hammer of wind,
And His graver of frost.'

WINTER-PIECE

You wake, all windows blind – embattled sprays
grained on the medieval glass.
Gates snap like gunshot
as you handle them. Five-barred fragility
sets flying fifteen rooks who go together
silently ravenous about this winter-piece
that will not feed them. They alight
beyond, scavenging, missing everything
but the bladed atmosphere, the white resistance.
Ruts with iron flanges track
through a hard decay
where you discern once more
oak-leaf by hawthorn, for the frost
rewhets their edges. In a perfect web
blanched along each spoke
and circle of its woven wheel,
the spider hangs, grasp unbroken
and death-masked in cold. Returning
you see the house glint-out behind
its holed and ragged glaze,
frost-fronds all streaming.

Walt Whitman 1819–92

'I THINK I COULD TURN AND LIVE WITH ANIMALS'

From 'Song of Myself'

I think I could turn and live with animals, they are so placid
     and self-contain'd,
I stand and look at them long and long.

They do not sweat and whine about their condition,
They do not lie awake in the dark and weep for their sins,
They do not make me sick discussing their duty to God,
Not one is dissatisfied, not one is demented with the mania
     of owning things,
Not one kneels to another, nor to his kind that lived
     thousands of years ago,
Not one is respectable or unhappy over the whole earth.

_____

MAUD MULLER

Maud Muller on a summer's day,
Raked the meadow sweet with hay.

Beneath her torn hat glowed the wealth
Of simple beauty and rustic health.

Singing, she wrought, and her merry glee
The mock-bird echoed from his tree.

But when she glanced to the far-off town,
White from its hill-slope looking down,

The sweet song died, and a vague unrest
And a nameless longing filled her breast, –

A wish that she hardly dared to own,
For something better than she had known.

The Judge rode slowly down the lane,
Smoothing his horse's chestnut mane.

He drew his bridle in the shade
Of the apple-trees, to greet the maid,

And asked a draught from the spring that flowed
Through the meadow across the road.

She stooped where the cool spring bubbled up,
And filled for him her small tin cup,

And blushed as she gave it, looking down
On her feet so bare, and her tattered gown.

'Thanks!' said the Judge; 'a sweeter draught
From a fairer hand was never quaffed.'

He spoke of the grass and flowers and trees,
Of the singing birds and the humming bees;

Then talked of the haying, and wondered whether
The cloud in the west would bring foul weather.

And Maud forgot her brier-torn gown,
And her graceful ankles bare and brown;

And listened, while a pleased surprise
Looked from her long-lashed hazel eyes.

At last, like one who for delay
Seeks a vain excuse, he rode away.

Maud Muller looked and sighed: 'Ah me!
That I the Judge's bride might be!

'He would dress me up in silks so fine,
And praise and toast me at his wine.

'My father should wear a broadcloth coat;
My brother should sail a painted boat.

'I'd dress my mother so grand and gay,
And the baby should have a new toy each day.

'And I'd feed the hungry and clothe the poor,
And all should bless me who left our door.'

The Judge looked back as he climbed the hill,
And saw Maud Muller standing still.

'A form more fair, a face more sweet,
Ne'er hath it been my lot to meet.

'And her modest answer and graceful air
Show her wise and good as she is fair.

'Would she were mine, and I to-day,
Like her, a harvester of hay;

'No doubtful balance of rights and wrongs,
Nor weary lawyers with endless tongues,

'But low of cattle and song of birds,
And health and quiet and loving words.'

But he thought of his sisters, proud and cold,
And his mother, vain of her rank and gold.

So, closing his heart, the Judge rode on,
And Maud was left in the field alone.

But the lawyers smiled that afternoon,
When he hummed in court an old love-tune;

And the young girl mused beside the well
Till the rain on the unraked clover fell.

He wedded a wife of richest dower,
Who lived for fashion, as he for power.

Yet oft, in his marble hearth's bright glow,
He watched a picture come and go;

And sweet Maud Muller's hazel eyes
Looked out in their innocent surprise.

Oft, when the wine in his glass was red,
He longed for the wayside well instead;

And closed his eyes on his garnished rooms
To dream of meadows and clover-blooms.

And the proud man sighed, with a secret pain,
'Ah, that I were free again!

'Free as when I rode that day,
Where the barefoot maiden raked her hay.'

She wedded a man unlearned and poor,
And many children played round her door.

But care and sorrow, and childbirth pain,
Left their traces on heart and brain.

And oft, when the summer sun shone hot
On the new-mown hay in the meadow lot,

And she heard the little spring brook fall
Over the roadside, through the wall,

In the shade of the apple-tree again
She saw a rider draw his rein;

And, gazing down with timid grace,
She felt his pleased eyes read her face.

Sometimes her narrow kitchen walls
Stretched away into stately halls;

The weary wheel to a spinnet turned,
The tallow candle an astral burned,

And for him who sat by the chimney lug,
Dozing and grumbling o'er pipe and mug,

A manly form at her side she saw,
And joy was duty and love was law.

Then she took up her burden of life again,
Saying only, 'It might have been.'

Alas for maiden, alas for Judge,
For rich repiner and household drudge!

God pity them both! and pity us all,
Who vainly the dreams of youth recall.

For of all sad words of tongue or pen,
The saddest are these: 'It might have been!'

Ah, well! for us all some sweet hope lies
Deeply buried from human eyes;

And, in the hereafter, angels may
Roll the stone from its grave away!

1854

Oscar Wilde 1854–1900

From 'THE BALLAD OF READING GAOL'

1

He did not wear his scarlet coat,
    For blood and wine are red,
And blood and wine were on his hands
    When they found him with the dead,
The poor dead woman whom he loved,
    and murdered in her bed.

He walked amongst the Trial Men
    In a suit of shabby grey;
A cricket cap was on his head,
    And his step seemed light and gay;
But I never saw a man who looked
    So wistfully at the day.

I never saw a man who looked
    With such a wistful eye
Upon that little tent of blue
    Which prisoners call the sky,
And at every drifting cloud that went
    With sails of silver by.

I walked, with other souls in pain,
    Within another ring,
And was wondering if the man had done
    A great or little thing,
When a voice behind me whispered low,
    'That fellow's got to swing.'

Dear Christ! the very prison walls
    Suddenly seemed to reel,
And the sky above my head became
    Like a casque of scorching steel;
And, though I was a soul in pain,
    My pain I could not feel.

I only knew what hunted thought
    Quickened his step, and why
He looked upon the garish day
    With such a wistful eye;
The man had killed the thing he loved,
    And so he had to die.

*

Yet each man kills the thing he loves,
    By each let this be heard,
Some do it with a bitter look,
    Some with a flattering word.
The coward does it with a kiss,
    The brave man with a sword!

Some kill their love when they are young,
    And some when they are old;
Some strangle with the hands of Lust,
    Some with the hands of Gold:
The kindest use a knife, because
    The dead so soon grow cold.

Some love too little, some too long,
    Some sell, and others buy;
Some do the deed with many tears,
    And some without a sigh:
For each man kills the thing he loves,
    Yet each man does not die.

He does not die a death of shame
    On a day of dark disgrace,
Nor have a noose about his neck,
    Nor a cloth upon his face,
Nor drop feet foremost through the floor
    Into an empty space.

He does not sit with silent men
    Who watch him night and day;
Who watch him when he tries to weep,
    And when he tries to pray;
Who watch him lest himself should rob
    The prison of its prey.

He does not wake at dawn to see
    Dread figures throng his room,
The shivering Chaplain robed in white,
    The Sheriff stern with gloom,
And the Governor all in shiny black,
    With the yellow face of Doom.

He does not rise in piteous hate
    To put on convict-clothes,
While some coarse-mouthed Doctor gloats, and notes
    Each new and nerve-twitched pose,
Fingering a watch whose little ticks
    Are like horrible hammer-blows.

He does not feel that sickening thirst
    That sands one's throat, before
The hangman with his gardener's gloves
    Comes through the padded door,
And binds one with three leathern thongs,
    That the throat may thirst no more.

He does not bend his head to hear
    The Burial Office read,
Nor, while the anguish of his soul
    Tells him he is not dead,
Cross his own coffin, as he moves
    Into the hideous shed.

He does not stare upon the air
    Through a little roof of glass:
He does not pray with lips of clay
    For his agony to pass;
Nor feel upon his shuddering cheek
    The kiss of Caiaphas.

2

Six weeks the guardsman walked the yard,
    In the suit of shabby grey:
His cricket cap was on his head,
    And his step seemed light and gay,
But I never saw a man who looked
    So wistfully at the day.

I never saw a man who looked
    With such a wistful eye
Upon that little tent of blue
    Which prisoners call the sky,
And at every wandering cloud that trailed
    Its ravelled fleeces by.

He did not wring his hands, as do
    Those witless men who dare
To try to rear the changeling Hope
    In the cave of black Despair:
He only looked upon the sun,
    And drank the morning air.

He did not wring his hands nor weep,
    Nor did he peek or pine,
But he drank the air as though it held
    Some healthful anodyne;
With open mouth he drank the sun
    As though it had been wine!

And I and all the souls in pain,
    Who tramped the other ring,
Forgot if we ourselves had done
    A great or little thing,
And watched with gaze of dull amaze
    The man who had to swing.

For strange it was to see him pass
    With a step so light and gay,
And strange it was to see him look
    So wistfully at the day,
And strange it was to think that he
    Had such a debt to pay.

William Wordsworth 1770–1850

COMPOSED UPON WESTMINSTER BRIDGE, SEPTEMBER 3, 1802

Earth has not anything to show more fair:
Dull would he be of soul who could pass by
A sight so touching in its majesty:
This City now doth, like a garment, wear
The beauty of the morning: silent, bare,
Ships, towers, domes, theatres, and temples lie
Open unto the fields, and to the sky;
All bright and glittering in the smokeless air.
Never did sun more beautifully steep
In his first splendour, valley, rock, or hill;
Ne'er saw I, never felt, a calm so deep!
The river glideth at his own sweet will:
Dear God! the very houses seem asleep;
And all that mighty heart is lying still!

Sir Henry Wotton 1568–1639

CHARACTER OF A HAPPY LIFE

How happy is he born and taught
That serveth not another's will;
Whose armour is his honest thought
And simple truth his utmost skill!

Whose passions not his masters are,
Whose soul is still prepared for death,
Not tied unto the world with care
Of public fame, or private breath;

Who envies none that chance doth raise
Or vice; Who never understood
How deepest wounds are given by praise;
Nor rules of state, but rules of good:

Who hath his life from rumours freed,
Whose conscience is his strong retreat;
Whose state can neither flatterers feed,
Nor ruin make oppressors great;

Who God doth late and early pray
More of his grace than gifts to lend;
And entertains the harmless day
With a well-chosen book or friend;

– This man is freed from servile bands
Of hope to rise, or fear to fall;
Lord of himself, though not of lands;
And having nothing, yet hath all.

W. B. Yeats 1865–1939

A PRAYER FOR MY DAUGHTER

Once more the storm is howling, and half hid
Under this cradle-hood and coverlid
My child sleeps on. There is no obstacle
But Gregory's wood and one bare hill
Whereby the haystack- and roof-levelling wind,
Bred on the Atlantic, can be stayed;
And for an hour I have walked and prayed
Because of the great gloom that is in my mind.

I have walked and prayed for this young child an hour
And heard the sea-wind scream upon the tower,
And under the arches of the bridge, and scream
In the elms above the flooded stream;
Imagining in excited reverie
That the future years had come,
Dancing to a frenzied drum,
Out of the murderous innocence of the sea.

May she be granted beauty and yet not
Beauty to make a stranger's eye distraught,
Or hers before a looking-glass, for such,
Being made beautiful overmuch,
Consider beauty a sufficient end,
Lose natural kindness and maybe
The heart-revealing intimacy
That chooses right, and never find a friend.

Helen being chosen found life flat and dull
And later had much trouble from a fool,
While that great Queen, that rose out of the spray,

Being fatherless could have her way
Yet chose a bandy-leggèd smith for man.
It's certain that fine women eat
A crazy salad with their meat
Whereby the Horn of Plenty is undone.

In courtesy I'd have her chiefly learned;
Hearts are not had as a gift but hearts are earned
By those that are not entirely beautiful;
Yet many, that have played the fool
For beauty's very self, has charm made wise,
And many a poor man that has roved,
Loved and thought himself beloved,
From a glad kindness cannot take his eyes.

May she become a flourishing hidden tree
That all her thoughts may like the linnet be,
And have no business but dispensing round
Their magnanimities of sound,
Nor but in merriment begin a chase,
Nor but in merriment a quarrel.
O may she live like some green laurel
Rooted in one dear perpetual place.

My mind, because the minds that I have loved,
The sort of beauty that I have approved,
Prosper but little, has dried up of late,
Yet knows that to be choked with hate
May well be of all evil chances chief.
If there's no hatred in a mind
Assault and battery of the wind
Can never tear the linnet from the leaf.

An intellectual hatred is the worst,
So let her think opinions are accursed.
Have I not seen the loveliest woman born
Out of the mouth of Plenty's horn,
Because of her opinionated mind
Barter that horn and every good
By quiet natures understood
For an old bellows full of angry wind?

Considering that, all hatred driven hence,
The soul recovers radical innocence
And learns at last that it is self-delighting,
Self-appeasing, self-affrighting,
And that its own sweet will is Heaven's will;
She can, though every face should scowl
And every windy quarter howl
Or every bellows burst, be happy still.

And may her bridegroom bring her to a house
Where all's accustomed, ceremonious;
For arrogance and hatred are the wares
Peddled in the thoroughfares.
How but in custom and in ceremony
Are innocence and beauty born?
Ceremony's a name for the rich horn,
And custom for the spreading laurel tree.

Index of First Lines

ACKNOWLEDGEMENTS

The Publishers would like to acknowledge the following for permission to reproduce copyright material:

Dannie Abse for 'The Mountaineers' from *Tenants of the House; Poems 1951-56* (Hutchinson), © Dannie Abse; Faber and Faber Ltd for 'Lullaby' from *Collected Shorter Poems 1927-57* by W. H. Auden; Curtis Brown & John Farquharson for 'Christmas' by Sir John Betjeman; Mrs Nicolete Gray and The Society of Authors on behalf of the Laurence Binyon Estate for 'The Little Dancers' by Laurence Binyon; Peters Fraser & Dunlop Group Ltd for 'Forefathers' by Edmund Blunden from *Poems of Many Years* (William Collins Sons & Co. Ltd); Francisco Campbell and Ad. Donker (Pty) Ltd for 'Horses on the Camargue' by Roy Campbell; Charles Causley for 'I Am the Great Sun' from *Collected Poems of Charles Causley* (Macmillan); Faber and Faber Ltd for 'Engineers' Corner' from *Making Cocoa for Kingsley Amis* by Wendy Cope; Random Century Group for 'To a Fat Lady Seen from the Train' from *Yesterday and Today* (The Cresset Press) by Frances Cornford; Faber and Faber Ltd for 'Skimbleshanks: The Railway Cat' from *Old Possums Book of Practical Cats* by T. S. Eliot; The Estate of Robert Frost for 'After Apple-Picking' from *The Poetry of Robert Frost*, edited by Edward Connery Lathem (Jonathan Cape); Faber and Faber Ltd for 'Digging' from *Death of a Naturalist* by Seamus Heaney; Faber and Faber Ltd for 'Hawk Roosting' from *Lupercal* by Ted Hughes; Emyr Humphreys for 'From Father to Son'; Elizabeth Jennings for 'Song at the Beginning of Autumn' from *Collected Poems of Elizabeth Jennings* (Macmillan); P. J. Kavanagh for 'News from Gloucestershire'; Marvell Press for 'Church Going' from *The Less Deceived* by Philip Larkin; Peters Fraser & Dunlop Group Ltd for 'Home from Abroad' by Laurie Lee; Norman MacCaig for 'Sparrow' from *Norman MacCaig: Collected Poems* (Hogarth Press); Charles Mackenzie for 'Macallister Dances Before the King' by D. M. Mackenzie; David Higham Associates Ltd for 'Apple Blossom' from *Collected Poems of Louis MacNeice* (Faber and Faber Ltd); The Literary Trustees of Walter de la Mare and The Society of Authors as their representative for 'Silver' by Walter de la Mare; The Society of Authors as the literary representative of the Estate of John Masefield for 'The West Wind' by John Masefield; Peters Fraser & Dunlop Group Ltd for 'At Lunchtime' by Roger McGough; Octopus Childrens Publishing for 'The King's Breakfast' by A. A. Milne from *When we were Very Young* (Methuen Childrens Books); John Murray (Publishers) Ltd for 'Wizardry' © Alfred Noyes 1963, from *Collected Poems of Alfred Noyes*; David Higham Associates Ltd for 'The Cocky Walkers' by Mervyn Peake from *Poems of our Time* (Dent); Irina Ratushinskaya for 'I Will Live and Survive' from *No, I'm not Afraid*, translated by David McDuff (Bloodaxe Books 1986); Simon Rae for 'Poetry Please!' poem; Curtis Brown & John Farquharson on behalf of the author's estate for 'The Greater Cats' by Vita Sackville-West; George T. Sassoon for 'Secret Music' by Siegfried Sassoon; Vernon Scannell for 'After the Fireworks'; John Smith for 'Nevertheless; James MacGibbon for 'The Singing Cat' by Stevie Smith from *Collected Poems of Stevie Smith* (Penguin Twentieth Century Classics); Peters Fraser & Dunlop Group Ltd for 'The Truly Great' by Sir Stephen Spender; The Society of Authors on behalf of the copyright owner, Mrs Iris Wise, for 'In the Poppy Field' by James Stephens; Hubert Nicholson for 'Cats' by A. S. J. Tessimond; David Higham Associates Ltd for 'The Force that Through the Green Fuse Drives the Flower' by Dylan Thomas from *The Poems of Dylan Thomas* (Dent); Charles Tomlinson for 'Winter Piece'.

The Publishers have made every effort to trace copyright holders of material reproduced within this compilation. If, however, they have inadvertently made any error they would be grateful for notification.